D.R. Browning, B
F.R.S.C., A.R.T.C

Principal Lecturer and Head
Polytechnic

Digital techniques
Level 2

Longman   London and New York

Longman Group Limited
Longman House, Burnt Mill, Harlow
Essex CM20 2JE, England
Associated companies throughout the world

*Published in the United States of America
by Longman Inc., New York*

First published 1984

British Library Cataloguing in Publication Data

Browning, D.R.
 Digital techniques Level 2. – (Longman Technician
 Series)
 1. Digital electronics
 I. Title   II. Series
 621.3815   TK7868.D5

 ISBN 0-582-41289-7

Set in 10/11 Linotron 202 Times
Printed in Hong Kong by
Astros Printing Ltd

Longman Technician Series

Mathematics and Sciences

Sector Editor:

D.R. Browning, B.Sc., C. Chem., F.R.S.C., A.R.T.C.S.
Principal Lecturer and Head of Chemistry, Bristol Polytechnic

Books already published in this sector of the series:

Technician mathematics Level 1 Second edition   *J O Bird and A J C May*
Technician mathematics Level 2 Second edition   *J O Bird and A J C May*
Technician mathematics Level 3   *J O Bird and A J C May*
Technician mathematics Levels 4 and 5   *J O Bird and A J C May*
Mathematics for electrical and telecommunications technicians *J O Bird and A J C May*
Mathematics for science technicians Level 2   *J O Bird and A J C May*
Mathematics for electrical technicians Level 3   *J O Bird and A J C May*
Mathematics for electrical technicians Levels 4 and 5   *J O Bird and A J C May*
Calculus for technicians   *J O Bird and A J C May*
Statistics for technicians   *J O Bird and A J C May*
Algebra for technicians   *J O Bird and A J C May*
Physical sciences Level 1   *D R Browning and I McKenzie Smith*
Engineering science for technicians Level 1   *D R Browning and I McKenzie Smith*
Safety science for technicians   *W J Hackett and G P Robbins*
Technician chemistry Level 1   *J Brockington and P J Stamper*
Fundamentals of chemistry   *J H J Peet*
Further studies in chemistry   *J H J Peet*
Organic chemistry for higher education   *J Brockington and P J Stamper*
Inorganic chemistry for higher education   *J Brockington and P J Stamper*
Cell biology for technicians   *N A Thorpe*
Mathematics for scientific and technical students   *H G Davies and G A Hicks*
Mathematical formulae for TEC courses   *J O Bird and A J C May*
Science formulae for TEC courses   *D R Browning*
Microprocessor appreciation   *J F A Thompson*
Technician physics Level 2   *E Deeson*

Contents

Preface

Preface

The text-book is primarily designed to meet the requirements of the Business and Technician Education Council Level II Digital Techniques half unit. However, it has been widened in scope slightly to provide a general introduction to the subject for those who require a basic knowledge of Binary Arithmetic, Boolean Algebra and Logic.

It assumes no knowledge of the subject and is dealt with in sufficient detail that this coupled with a wealth of worked and unworked examples, should enable the student to study the topic in an Open Learning situation if required.

The author would like to thank colleagues, in particular Eric Deeson and Terry Pick for their advice during the preparation of the book and for correcting the original work. Finally, thanks are due to Val Serjeant for her patient and accurate typing of a rather difficult manuscript.

David BROWNING   Bristol Polytechnic, 1983

Chapter 1

Denary binary and octal number systems

1.1 Introduction

In our everyday lives the calculations we have to do involve the use of a system of numbers from 0 to 9, i.e. 0, 1, 2, 3, 4, 5, 6, 7, 8, 9 and we can obtain any number by a suitable combination of these. This system of numbering is called the *denary system*.

However, many calculations are now carried out using digital computers which are constructed from two-state devices such as ON-OFF switches. The OFF position is represented by the number 0 and the ON position by the number 1. Calculations using digital computers involve a system consisting of only two numbers. This system of numbering is called the *binary system*.

Since most of our calculations are carried out in the denary system and the digital computer can only work in the binary system, this gives rise to three problems:

(1) a need to convert denary numbers to binary numbers;
(2) a need to be able to carry out all arithmetical operations in binary numbers in a way which is compatible with the computer;
(3) a need to convert the answer, obtained in the binary system, back to the denary system.

The first three chapters are devoted to showing how these problems can be solved. In this chapter we are concerned with problems 1 and 3, i.e. the conversion of numbers from one system to another.

1.2 The denary and binary systems

All numbers in the denary system are built up in the same way, e.g.

$$329 = 300 + 20 + 9$$
$$= 3 \times 100 + 2 \times 10 + 9$$

It can be seen from this that the number on the extreme right tells us how many units there are (9 in this case). The number one place to the left of this (2 in this case) tells us how many tens there are and that two places to the left (3 in this case) how many hundreds. The number on the extreme right is known as the *least significant digit* and that on the extreme left as the *most significant digit*.

In the same way $82\,641 = 8 \times 10\,000 + 2 \times 1\,000 + 6 \times 100 + 4 \times 10 + 1 \times 1$ where 8 is the most significant digit and 1 is the least significant digit. Now $100 = 10^2$, $1\,000 = 10^3$, $10\,000 = 10^4$ and so on. Similarly $10 = 10^1$ and $1 = 10^0$.

Therefore the above numbers can be written in the form

$$329 = 3 \times 10^2 + 2 \times 10^1 + 9 \times 10^0 \text{ and}$$
$$82\,641 = 8 \times 10^4 + 2 \times 10^3 + 6 \times 10^2 + 4 \times 10^1 + 1 \times 10^0$$

Each digit in the above numbers represents that digit multiplied by ten to a suitable power. The denary system is said to have a *base, modulus* or *radix* of ten. In any chosen number the power of 10 *increases* from right to left. In the above numbers each part is split up into two:

(1) a number from 0 to 9 which is called the mantissa, e.g. 3 2 9
(2) ten to a given power which is called the exponent, e.g. 10^2 10^1 10^0

In the binary system there are only two digits, 0 and 1. This system has a base of 2, e.g.

$$1101 = 1 \times 2^3 + 1 \times 2^2 + 0 \times 2^1 + 1 \times 2^0$$

In the same way as before the power of 2 increases from right to left. The numbers 0 and 1 are known as Binary digITS (or BITS). The bit at the extreme right-hand side of the number is known as the least significant bit and that at the extreme left-hand side as the most significant bit.

$$1101 = 1 \times 2^3 + 1 \times 2^2 + 0 \times 2^1 + 1 \times 2^0$$
$$= 8 + 4 + 0 + 1 = 13$$

Therefore a binary number is readily converted to a denary number.

A table of binary numbers is given in Table 1.1

It is readily seen that the pattern is easily built up. Since the repeat pattern has the same number of 0's and 1's given by the corresponding exponent, the next line in Table 1.2 should be 2^4, that is 16 0's followed by 16 1's and so on.

Table 1.1

Denary number	Binary number			
	2^3 $1 \times 2^3 \quad 0 \times 2^3$	2^2 $1 \times 2^2 \quad 0 \times 2^2$	2^1 $1 \times 2^1 \quad 0 \times 2^1$	2^0 $1 \times 2^0 \quad 0 \times 2^0$
0	0	0	0	0
1	0	0	0	1
2	0	0	1	0
3	0	0	1	1
4	0	1	0	0
5	0	1	0	1
6	0	1	1	0
7	0	1	1	1
8	1	0	0	0
9	1	0	0	1
10	1	0	1	0
11	1	0	1	1
12	1	1	0	0
13	1	1	0	1
14	1	1	1	0
15	1	1	1	1

Table 1.2

Column 2^0	repeat pattern is 01	i.e. $1(2^0)$, 0 and 1,1
2^1	repeat pattern is 0011	$2(2^1)$, 0's and 2,1's
2^2	repeat pattern is 00001111	$4(2^2)$, 0's and 4,1's
2^3	repeat pattern is 0000000011111111	$8(2^3)$, 0's and 8,1's

1.3 Decimal and binary fractions

All fractions can be represented in the same way as before using negative powers of the appropriate base.

For example $0.487 = \dfrac{4}{10} + \dfrac{8}{100} + \dfrac{7}{1000}$

$\qquad\qquad\qquad = 4 \times 10^{-1} + 8 \times 10^{-2} + 7 \times 10^{-3}$

In the same way the compound number

$142.65 = 1 \times 10^2 + 4 \times 10^1 + 2 \times 10^0 + 6 \times 10^{-1} + 5 \times 10^{-2}$

In the binary system

$0.11111 \quad = 1 \times 2^{-1} + 1 \times 2^{-2} + 1 \times 2^{-3} + 1 \times 2^{-4} + 1 \times 2^{-5}$

$\qquad\qquad = \dfrac{1}{2} + \dfrac{1}{4} + \dfrac{1}{8} + \dfrac{1}{16} + \dfrac{1}{32} = \dfrac{31}{32}$ in denary form

Similarly, the compound number

$$1101.0101 = 1 \times 2^3 + 1 \times 2^2 + 0 \times 2^1 + 1 \times 2^0 + 0 \times 2^{-1} + 1 \times 2^{-2} + 0 \times 2^{-3} + 1 \times 2^{-4}$$
$$= 8 + 4 + 0 + 1 + 0 + \frac{1}{4} + 0 + \frac{1}{16} = 13\frac{5}{16} \text{ in denary form}$$

1.4 Conversion of denary into binary numbers

An easy method of converting whole numbers (called integers) from the denary to the binary system is outlined below.

Convert 432 to binary form.   This is done by repeatedly dividing by two. The remainders numbering from bottom to top give the binary number.

2	432	
2	216	remainder 0
2	108	remainder 0
2	54	remainder 0
2	27	remainder 0
2	13	remainder 1
2	6	remainder 1
2	3	remainder 0
2	1	remainder 1
	0	remainder 1

Therefore the resulting binary number reading from bottom to top is 110110000
This can be checked as follows:

$$110110000 = 1 \times 2^8 + 1 \times 2^7 + 0 \times 2^6 + 1 \times 2^5 + 1 \times 2^4 + 0 \times 2^3 + 0 \times 2^2 + 0 \times 2^1 + 0 \times 2^0$$
$$= 256 + 128 + 32 + 16 = 432$$

Fractional numbers on the binary system contain exponents with negative powers.

For example $0.1111 = 1 \times 2^{-1} + 1 \times 2^{-2} + 1 \times 2^{-3} + 1 \times 2^{-4}$
$$= 1 \times \frac{1}{2^1} + 1 \times \frac{1}{2^2} + 1 \times \frac{1}{2^3} + 1 \times \frac{1}{2^4}$$

Each digit *measured from the point* and *going to the right decreases* by a power of two. For *whole numbers* each digit *measured from the point* and *going to the left increases* by a power of two.

When converting fractions from the denary to the binary form we therefore reverse the procedure adopted for whole numbers, i.e.:

(1) we multiply repeatedly by two instead of dividing;
(2) we read the answer from top to bottom instead of bottom to top.

Note: When multiplying, multiply only the figures to the right of the point in each case.

Convert 0.643 from denary to binary form.

$$
\begin{array}{l}
0.643 \\
\times 2 \\
\hline
1.286 \\
\times 2 \\
\hline
0.572 \\
\times 2 \\
\hline
1.144 \\
\times 2 \\
\hline
0.288 \\
\times 2 \\
\hline
0.576
\end{array}
$$

As with decimal fractions we have to take our results to a definite number of binary places to give us the degree of accuracy we require. In the above example 0.643 = 0.10100 to five binary places. The answer can be checked as follows:

$$0.10100 = 1 \times 2^{-1} + 0 \times 2^{-2} + 1 \times 2^{-3} + 0 \times 2^{-4} + 0 \times 2^{-5}$$
$$= \frac{1}{2} + \frac{1}{8}$$
$$= 0.5 + 0.125 = 0.625$$

The inaccuracy in the answer is because we have not carried the multiplication far enough. Let us take it a little further.

$$
\begin{array}{l}
0.576 \\
\times 2 \\
\hline
1.152 \\
\times 2 \\
\hline
0.204
\end{array}
$$

The answer to seven binary places is now 0.1010010.

Checking as before

$$0.1010010 = [0.625] + 1 \times 2^{-6} + 0 \times 2^{-7}$$
$$= 0.625 + \frac{1}{64}$$
$$= 0.625 + 0.016 = 0.641$$

This answer is much closer to the real answer and as with decimal fractions the accuracy will increase the more places we choose.

Compound numbers are treated as shown below.

Convert 147.5625 to binary form. Separate the number into the integer 147 and fraction 0.5625. Divide 147 repeatedly by 2 and multiply 0.5625 repeatedly by two.

2	147	
2	73	remainder 1
2	36	1
2	18	0
2	9	0
2	4	1
2	2	0
2	1	0
	0	1

```
  0 .5625
        2
 1 .1250
        2
 0 .250
        2
 0 .50
        2
 1 .0
```

The answer is 10010011.1001

Check

$$10010011.1001 = 1 \times 2^7 + 1 \times 2^4 + 1 \times 2^1 + 1 \times 2^0 + 1 \times 2^{-1} + 1 \times 2^{-4}$$
$$= 128 + 16 + 2 + 1 + \frac{1}{2} + \frac{1}{16}$$
$$= 147 + 0.5 + 0.0625$$
$$= 147.5625$$

When a compound number is converted to binary form the answer is not always exact, i.e. the remainder is not always zero, as shown above. For example, if we convert 172.91 to binary form we obtain

```
2 | 172
2 |  86   0  ↑
2 |  43   0
2 |  21   1
2 |  10   1
2 |   5   0
2 |   2   1
2 |   1   0
       0   1
```

```
     0 .91
         2
     1 .82
         2
     1 .64
         2
     1 .28
         2
     0 .56
         2
     1 .12
         2
  ↓  0 .24
```

If we now look at the fractional portion of the answer we see that there is still a remainder even if the number is taken to six binary places. Therefore the number in binary form is not exactly equal to that in denary form. Let us examine this fractional value further. If the number is taken correct to three binary places (i.e. three places after the point) then

$$0.111 = 1 \times \frac{1}{2} + 1 \times \frac{1}{4} + 1 \times \frac{1}{8}$$
$$= 0.5 + 0.25 + 0.125$$
$$= 0.875$$

Since the fourth binary place is 0, this extra figure gives the same answer as for three places. However the fifth binary figure is 1 and it is easily confirmed that

$$0.11101 = 0.875 + 0 \times \frac{1}{16} + 1 \times \frac{1}{32}$$
$$= 0.875 + 0 + 0.031\ 25$$
$$= 0.906\ 25$$

This latter value is much closer to the correct answer of 0.91 than is 0.875. The more figures we take after the point the more nearly correct is our answer. We can say that the answer is 10101100.11101 to five binary places.

One problem might arise as shown in the following example.

Convert 111 in denary form to binary form

2	111		
2	55	remainder 1	
2	27	1	
2	13	1	
2	6	1	
2	3	0	
2	1	1	
	0	1	

Therefore 111 in denary form is 1101111 in binary form. It is possible that confusion may arise as to which system these numbers are in. This can be eliminated by using the suffix 10 for the denary system and suffix 2 for the binary system as shown below.

$$111_{10} = 1101111_2 \text{ or } (111)_{10} = (1101111)_2$$

Check

$$1101111_2 = 1 \times 2^6 + 1 \times 2^5 + 1 \times 2^3 + 1 \times 2^2 + 1 \times 2^1 + 1 \times 2^0$$
$$= 64_{10} + 32_{10} + 8_{10} + 4_{10} + 2_{10} + 1_{10} = 111_{10}$$

Worked examples 1.4

Example 1   Convert 53_{10} to binary form

Answer

2	53		
2	26	remainder 1	
2	13	0	
2	6	1	
2	3	0	
2	1	1	
	0	1	

Therefore $53_{10} = 110101_2$

Check 110101 $= 1 \times 2^5 + 1 \times 2^4 + 1 \times 2^2 + 1 \times 2^0$
$= 32 + 16 + 4 + 1 = 53$

Example 2 Express 0.15625_{10} in binary form to six binary places

Answer

$$
\begin{array}{r}
0.15625 \\
2 \\
\hline
0\,|.31250 \\
2 \\
\hline
0\,|.6250 \\
2 \\
\hline
1\,|.250 \\
2 \\
\hline
0\,|.50 \\
2 \\
\hline
1\,|.0 \\
2 \\
\hline
0\,|.0
\end{array}
$$

Therefore $0.156\,25_{10} = 0.001010_2$ to six binary places

Check $0.001010_2 = 1 \times 2^{-3} + 1 \times 2^{-5}$
$$= \frac{1}{8} + \frac{1}{32} = 0.125 + 0.03125 = 0.15625$$

Example 3 Convert 163.84_{10} to binary form

Answer

2	163	
2	81	remainder 1
2	40	1
2	20	0
2	10	0
2	5	0
2	2	1
2	1	0
	0	1

$$
\begin{array}{r}
0.84 \\
2 \\
\hline
1\,|.68 \\
2 \\
\hline
1\,|.36 \\
2 \\
\hline
0\,|.72 \\
2 \\
\hline
1\,|.44 \\
2 \\
\hline
0\,|.88
\end{array}
$$

Therefore $163.84_{10} = 10100011.11010_2$ to five binary places.

Check $10100011.11010_2 = 1 \times 2^7 + 1 \times 2^5 + 1 \times 2^1 + 1 \times 2^0 +$
$\qquad\qquad\qquad\qquad 1 \times 2^{-1} + 1 \times 2^{-2} + 1 \times 2^{-4}$

$$= 128 + 32 + 2 + 1 + \frac{1}{2} + \frac{1}{4} + \frac{1}{16}$$

$$= 163 + 0.5 + 0.25 + 0.062\ 5$$

$$= 163.812\ 5$$

It can be seen that if we take the answer to six binary places we add on 1/64.

Then the required number $\quad = 163.812\ 5 + 0.015\ 625$
$\qquad\qquad\qquad\qquad\qquad = 163.828\ 125$

which is closer to the real value of 163.84.

1.5 Conversion of binary into denary numbers

Several examples have already been encountered in the checks in section 1.4. Three more examples are given below.

Worked examples 1.5

Example 1 Express 11010110_2 in denary form

Answer $11010110_2 = 1 \times 2^7 + 1 \times 2^6 + 0 \times 2^5 + 1 \times 2^4 + 0 \times 2^3 +$
$\qquad\qquad\qquad 1 \times 2^2 + 1 \times 2^1 + 0 \times 2^0$
$\qquad\qquad\quad = 128 + 64 + 16 + 4 + 2 = 214_{10}$

Example 2 Convert 0.11011_2 to denary form

Answer $0.11011_2 \quad = 1 \times 2^{-1} + 1 \times 2^{-2} + 0 \times 2^{-3} + 1 \times 2^{-4} + 1 \times 2^{-5}$
$\qquad\qquad\quad = \frac{1}{2} + \frac{1}{4} + \frac{1}{16} + \frac{1}{32}$
$\qquad\qquad\quad = \frac{27}{32}_{10} \quad = \underline{0.843\ 75_{10}}$

Example 3 Express 10010011.101_2 in denary form

Answer $10010011.101_2 \quad = 1 \times 2^7 + 1 \times 2^4 + 1 \times 2^1 + 1 \times 2^0 + 1 \times 2^-$
$\qquad\qquad\qquad\qquad + 1 \times 2^{-3}$
$\qquad\qquad\qquad\qquad = 128 + 16 + 2 + 1 + \frac{1}{2} + \frac{1}{8}$
$\qquad\qquad\qquad\qquad = 147\tfrac{5}{8} = \underline{147.625_{10}}$

Check that the above answers are correct by using the methods of section 1.4.

1.6 The octal system

The octal system of numbers is frequently used in computer operations because of the ease of converting octal numbers into binary numbers by inspection.

It consists of the numbers 0 to 7 represented by three digit binary numbers as shown in Table 1.3 (compare with Table 1.1)

Table 1.3

octal numbers	binary numbers
0	000
1	001
2	010
3	011
4	100
5	101
6	110
7	111

This system has a base of 8 and numbers are represented in a manner similar to those in base 10 or base 2, e.g.:

$$1437_8 = 1 \times 8^3 + 4 \times 8^2 + 3 \times 8^1 + 7 \times 8^0 = 799_{10}$$

The number can be converted to base 2 by simply replacing the individual digits by the combinations given in Table 1.3, e.g.:

$$1437_8 = 001100011111_2$$

Fractions can be treated as before, e.g.:

$$1632.74_8 = 1 \times 8^3 + 6 \times 8^2 + 3 \times 8^1 + 2 \times 8^0 + 7 \times 8^{-1} + 4 \times 8^{-2}$$
$$= 512 + 384 + 24 + 2 + 0.875 + 0.0625 = 922.9375_{10}$$
$$= 000110011010.111100_2$$

Although these binary numbers appear to be cumbersome they are readily dealt with by computer.

When very large numbers have to be converted from the denary to the binary system, continuous division and multiplication by 2 can be very tedious. Conversion to the octal system means considerably fewer divisions and multiplications by 8. The conversion of octal to binary can then be done by inspection.

The method is conveniently shown in the following example.

Convert 1 789.65$_{10}$ to the binary system

$3375.514_8 = 011011111101.101001100_2$

Check

$$011011111101.101001100 = 1 \times 2^{10} + 1 \times 2^9 + 1 \times 2^7 + 1 \times 2^6 + 1 \times$$
$$+ 1 \times 2^4 + 1 \times 2^3 + 1 \times 2^2 + 1 \times 2^0 +$$
$$1 \times 2^{-1} + 1 \times 2^{-3} + 1 \times 2^{-6} + 1 \times 2^{-7}$$
$$= 1\ 024 + 512 + 128 + 64 + 32 + 16 + 8 +$$
$$4 + 1 + 0.5 + 0.125 + 0.015\ 625 +$$
$$0.007\ 812\ 5$$
$$= 1\ 789.648\ 4$$

Try this example by conversion directly to binary and compare the work involved in the calculation. It will be three times as long with greater possibility of error.

Exercise 1

Section 1.4

1. Convert the following numbers from the denary to the binary system: 39, 117, 298, 654, 1 029, 2 008, 721, 999, 672, 3 019
2. Convert the following decimal fractions to binary fractions: 0.75, 0.375, 0.062 5, 0.531 25, 0.093 75, 0.968 75, 0.187 5
3. Convert the following decimal fractions to binary fractions correct to five binary places:
0.86, 0.932, 0.785, 0.842, 0.196
4. Convert the denary numbers below into binary form correct to four binary places:
19.062 5, 24.968 75, 102.125, 231.97, 314.46, 642.35, 512.86

Section 1.5

5. Convert the following binary numbers to their corresponding denary numbers:
011, 101, 1111, 1011101, 1100011, 1000001, 11011101, 11111, 100111, 1110011

6. Convert the following binary fractions into decimal fractions:
   0.01, 0.110, 0.1011, 0.11101, 0.10001, 0.0001, 0.01101
7. Convert the compound binary numbers given below into the
   corresponding denary numbers:
   11.1, 101.101, 111.111, 1001.0011, 1010.1, 1000.1011, 11101.00001,
   1000.0001

Section 1.6

8. Carry out the conversions in question 4 by first converting to octal
   numbers.
9. Convert the following denary numbers into binary numbers:
   1 652.5, 4 739.81, 8 974.658
   by first converting them into octal numbers.

Chapter 2

The processes of binary arithmetic

2.1 Addition and subtraction of binary numbers

The methods of adding and subtracting numbers in the binary system are the same as those employed in the denary system but since only two numbers are involved the rules are much simpler.

Throughout the sections on binary arithmetic we will be comparing the binary processes with the corresponding ones in denary arithmetic. You should use these comparisons to improve your ability to convert from denary to binary and binary to denary numbers where appropriate.

(1) Addition
The rules of addition are

$0 + 0 = [0]\ 0$
$0 + 1 = [0]\ 1$
$1 + 0 = [0]\ 1$
$1 + 1 = [1]\ 0$

Using the above rules we can see that

$1 + 1 + 1 = [1]\ 0 + 1 = [1]\ 1$

The numbers in brackets are called carry bits and are always placed one place to the left (i.e. in the next higher order of 2) in binary arithmetic.

For example let us add the numbers 10010_2 and 11011_2. The two numbers to be added are known as the *augend* and the *addend*.

There is then a third and fourth row for the carry bits and the sum respectively.

augend	10010	18
addend	11011	27
	01001	35
carry	10010	1
sum	101101	45

Note: Terms such as augend and addend and minuend and subtrahend which appear later are not important at present but they are included since they will be met many times in later units.

The process is exactly the same for compound numbers as may be seen by adding 10.001_2 and 11.101_2.

augend	10.001	2.125
addend	11.101	3.625
	01.100	5.740
carry	100.01	0.01
sum	101.110	5.750

In some cases the carry process requires to be done more than once. Add 111.011_2 and 101.101_2.

augend	111.011	7.375
addend	101.101	5.625
	010.110	2.990
carry	1010.01	10.01
sum	1000.100	12.900
carry	00100.10	000.1
sum	1100.000	12.000
carry	00001.00	001.00
	1101.000	13.000

You would not normally carry out the addition of denary numbers in the detail shown. Much of this would be done mentally. In the same way you will carry out the repeated processes of binary addition mentally when more experienced in the technique.

(2) Subtraction

The rules of subtraction are

$$0 - 0 = [0]\ 0$$
$$1 - 0 = [0]\ 1$$
$$0 - 1 = [1]\ 1$$
$$1 - 1 = [0]\ 0$$

When 1 is subtracted from 0, 1 has to be borrowed from the next highest column. This 1 is equal to 2_{10} in this subtraction. Since $2-1$ is equal to 1 we have $0 - 1 = 1$ but we have to pay back 1 into the next highest column designated above by [1].

In subtraction the top line is known as the *minuend* and the bottom line as the *subtrahend*. If we subtract 01010_2 from 11101_2 we get

minuend	11101		29
subtrahend	01010		10
	10111		
pay back	00010		
difference	010011		19

As in the case of addition, repeated subtraction may be necessary. For example if we subtract 10010_2 from 11001_2 we obtain

minuend	11001	25
subtrahend	10010	18
	01011	17
pay back	00010	1
difference	1111	07
pay back	0100	
difference	00111	

Let us now consider the example $10101_2 - 11010_2$

minuend		10101	21
subtrahend		11010	26
		01111	
pay back		1010	
difference	[1]	11011	
subtract		⎿⟶1	
final difference		11010	−5

You will notice from the above calculation that:

(1) the answer in denary form is negative;
(2) an extra pay-back term [1] is obtained which is subtracted from the difference. The extra term [1] is there because the answer is negative.

However, it is clear that the binary number

11010 is not equal to 5
but   00101 is equal to 5

Therefore the value of 5 is obtained by converting all the 1's in the final difference to 0's and all the 0's to 1's. The number 00101 is called the *complement* of 11010 (see section 3.1). Compound numbers can be treated in exactly the same way as integers. For example, subtract 0101.101_2 from 1110.010_2.

minuend	1110.010	14.250
subtrahend	0101.101	5.625
	1011.111	19.635
pay back	0011 01	11 01
difference	1000.101	8.625

Worked examples 2.1

Example 1   Add 1101010_2 and 1010011_2

Answer	1101010	106
	1010011	83
	0111001	
	1000010	
	10111101	189

Example 2   Add 110.010_2 and 1001.101_2

Answer	110.010	6.25
	1001.101	9.625
	1111.111	
	0000 00	
	1111.111	15.875

Example 3   Add 1011.011_2 and 0110.101_2

Answer			more usually
	1011.011	11.375	11.375
	0110.101	6.625	6.625
	1101.110	17.990	18.000
	0100 01	00 01	1 11
	1001.100	17.900	
	1000 10	00 1	
	0001.000	17.000	
	10001 00	01	
	10000.000	18.000	
	00010 00		
	10010.000		

As in previous examples the decimal examples would be done as shown on the extreme right. With practice, binary examples can be done in the same way

```
  1011.011
  0110.101
 10010.000
  1111 11
```

Example 4   Subtract 01010_2 from 11101_2

Answer		
	11101	29
	01010	10
	10111	
	0010	
	10011	19

Example 5   Subtract 110001_2 from 101010_2

Answer		
	101010	42
	110001	49
	011011	
	10001	
[1]	111001	
	→1	
	111000	
Complement	= 000111	−07

Example 6 Subtract 1001.0111_2 from 1110.1010_2

Answer

1110.1010		14.6250
1001.0111		9.4375

0111.1101	15.2985
0010 101	10 111

101.0111	5.1875
000 01	

101.0011

As in example 3 we can use the following method:

1110.1010	14.6250
1001.0111	9.4375

0101.0011	5.1875

0010 111	10 111

2.2 Multiplication and division of binary numbers

Both multiplication and division can be carried out in exactly the same way as in denary arithmetic but the multiplication tables are much simpler. These are:

$0 \times 0 = 0$
$1 \times 0 = 0$
$0 \times 1 = 0$
$1 \times 1 = 1$

(1) Multiplication

Multiply 1011_2 by 101_2

1011		11
101		5

1011	⎫	
0000	⎬ partial products	
1011	⎭	

100111	
01000	

110111	55

The intermediate products in the multiplication are known as *partial products*. As in denary multiplication the insertion of the line multiplied by 0 serves no useful purpose.

An added complication is encountered when dealing with

computers. The digital computer can add only two lines of figures together at any one time.

In order to overcome the above difficulties the method used in the following example is normally employed.

Multiply 110101_2 by 10101_2

```
    110101
     10101
    110101    multiply top line by the 1 which is the least bit of the
              multiplier
   110101*    shift one place to the left to allow for ×0, then
              multiply by 1
 100001001    Add
 110101*      shift one place to the left to allow for ×0, then
              multiply by 1
10001011001   Add
```

In decimal notation

```
  53
  21
  ──
  53
 106
 ────
1113
```

Compound numbers can be treated in exactly the same way. For example, we multiply 101.11_2 by 11.101_2 as shown below. As in denary arithmetic the position of the point is determined by those in the two numbers being multiplied. In our example the point is $2 + 3 = 5$ places to the left of the least significant bit.

```
   101.11          5.75
   11.101          3.625
   ──────          ─────
   10 111          2 875
   1011 1*         11 50
   ──────          345 0
  1110 011         1725
  10111           ──────
  ─────────       20.8437 5
 100101 011
 10111
 ──────────
10100.11 011
```

Since this method consists of adding each pair of partial products and shifting to the left when multiplying by 0 it is sometimes called the *add and shift method*.

(2) Division

Divide 1010011011_2 by 11101_2

As in division using denary numbers we first divide 11101 into the same number of figures at the left-hand side of the number being divided (10100). Since 11101 is larger than 10100 it 'won't go'. Therefore we bring down the next number on the right which is 1.

Now 11101 does divide into 101001 once. On subtraction this gives 1100 and the next 1 is carried down. Since 11101 doesn't divide into 11001 put a '0' in the answer and carry down the next number from the number being divided. This is '0'.

11101 does divide into 110010 once. On subtraction this gives 10101. Division is continued as shown below.

The process is clearly the same as that used in denary arithmetic.

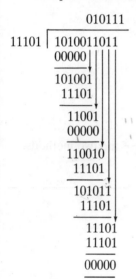

```
           010111                        23
    ┌──────────────            ┌─────────
11101 │ 1010011011          29 │ 667
        00000│││││                58
        ─────┘││││              ───
        101001││││                87
         11101││││                87
        ──────┘│││              ───
         11001 │││                00
         00000 │││              ───
        ───────┘││
         110010 ││
          11101 ││
         ───────┘│
          101011 │
           11101 │
          ───────┘
           11101
           11101
          ──────
           00000
```

The answer (called the *quotient*) is 10111_2.

As in denary division there may be a remainder. For example, if we divide 100011_2 by 1011_2

```
        11                    3
    ┌────────              ┌──────
1011 │ 100011          11 │ 35
       1011                 33
      ──────               ───
       1101                  2
       1011                ───
      ──────
         10
```

It can be seen that the binary remainder $10_2 = 2_{10}$.

Division of compound numbers is carried out in the same way.
For example, divide 100011.0011_2 by 1011_2

```
        11.0011                        3.1988
1011 │ 100011.0011          11 │ 35.1875
       1011                      33
       ────                      ──
       1101                      2 1
       1011                      1 1
       ────                      ───
       10 001                    1 08
        1 011                      99
        ─────                     ───
         1101                      97
         1011                      88
         ────                      ──
           10                      95
         ────                      88
                                   ──
                                    7
```

It can be seen that the denary equivalent of the
quotient 11.0011_2 = 3.1875_{10} ≠ 3.1988_{10}
remainder 10_2 = 2_{10} ≠ 7_{10}
The difference is due to a difference in accuracy of the two methods.

Worked examples 2.2

Example 1   Multiply 111_2 by 101_2

Answer   111   7
                     101   5
                     ───   ─
                     111
                    111*
                    ──────   ──
                    100011   35

Example 2   Multiply 1011_2 by 101101_2

Answer   1011   11
                   101101   45
                   ──────   ──
                     1011   55
                    1011*   44
                    ─────   ──
                   110111   495
                   1011
                   ──────
                  10001111
                  1011*
                  ─────────
                 111101111

Example 3   Multiply 101.1111_2 by 11.001_2

Answer

$$
\begin{array}{r}
101.1111 \\
11.001 \\
\hline
1011\ 111 \\
101\ 1111\ ** \\
\hline
110\ 1010\ 111 \\
1011\ 111 \\
\hline
10010.1000\ 111
\end{array}
\qquad
\begin{array}{r}
5.9375 \\
3.125 \\
\hline
29\ 6875 \\
118\ 750 \\
\hline
593\ 75 \\
17812\ 5 \\
\hline
18.554\ 6875
\end{array}
$$

Example 4   Divide 1111_2 by 101_2

Answer

$$
101\ \overline{\smash{)}\,1111} \quad\frac{11}{}
$$

$$
\begin{array}{r}
11 \\
101\ \overline{\smash{)}\,1111} \\
101 \\
\hline
101 \\
101 \\
\hline
000
\end{array}
\qquad
\begin{array}{r}
3 \\
9\ \overline{\smash{)}\,27} \\
27 \\
\hline
00
\end{array}
$$

The answer is 11_2 with no remainder.

Example 5   Divide 1011101_2 by 1100_2

Answer

$$
\begin{array}{r}
111 \\
1100\ \overline{\smash{)}\,1011101} \\
1100 \\
\hline
10110 \\
1100 \\
\hline
10101 \\
1100 \\
\hline
1001
\end{array}
\qquad
\begin{array}{r}
7 \\
12\ \overline{\smash{)}\,93} \\
84 \\
\hline
9
\end{array}
$$

Let us now continue this division further to remove the remainder.

$$
\begin{array}{r}
.11 \\
1100\ \overline{\smash{)}\,1001.00} \\
110\ 0 \\
\hline
011\ 00 \\
11\ 00 \\
\hline
00\ 00
\end{array}
\qquad
\begin{array}{r}
.75 \\
12\ \overline{\smash{)}\,9.0} \\
8\ 4 \\
\hline
60 \\
60 \\
\hline
00
\end{array}
$$

Therefore the answer is either 111_2 with a remainder of 1001_2 *or* 111.11_2 with no remainder, depending on how far the division is taken.

Example 6 Divide 10101110.1_2 by 10111_2 as far as the fourth binary place.

Answer

```
              111.1001                    7.5869
        ┌──────────────           ┌──────────────
  10111 │ 10101110.1000      23   │ 174.5000
          10111                     161
          ─────                     ───
          101001                    13 5
          10111                     11 5
          ─────                     ────
          100100                    2 00
          10111                     1 84
          ─────                     ────
          1101 1                    160
          1011 1                    138
          ──────                    ───
          10 0000                   220
          1 0111                    207
          ──────                    ───
          1001                      13
```

Note: $111.1001_2 = 7.5625_{10} \neq 7.5869_{10}$

The answers will become closer as more binary places are taken.

Exercise 2

All numbers in this section are binary numbers

Section 2.1

1. Evaluate

(1) 101 + 010
(2) 011 + 1100
(3) 110 + 101
(4) 1111 + 0101
(5) 1001 + 10101

(6) 11111 + 101011
(7) 10000 + 1011101
(8) 11101 + 10011
(9) 11111 + 1001100
(10) 101101 + 0011010

2. Evaluate

(1) 0.1101 + 0.0011
(2) 0.0001 + 0.1011
(3) 0.10101 + 0.11011

(4) 0.00101 + 0.11101
(5) 0.011101 + 0.111001
(6) 0.0001011 + 0.1010101

3. Evaluate

(1) 11.11 + 10.101
(2) 101.110 + 111.001
(3) 1111.111 + 1001.011

(4) 01101.1101 + 11001.0001
(5) 1011101.01011 + 10011.00101
(6) 11100011.00011 + 01011011.101101

4. Evaluate

(1) 11111 − 10100
(2) 10110 − 1001
(3) 11001 − 10110
(4) 10011 − 1101
(5) 1110011 − 1011101

(6) 10010 − 11011
(7) 11101 − 11110
(8) 100110 − 11001
(9) 1100011 − 1110100
(10) 10001 − 01011

5. Evaluate

(1) 11.11 − 10.01
(2) 110.101 − 011.001
(3) 1001.110 − 111.0011

(4) 110011.1001 − 1101.0110
(5) 111111.0001 − 101010.1111
(6) 100010.1 − 101.01011

Section 2.2

6. Evaluate

(1) $100_2 \times 010_2$
(2) $101_2 \times 11_2$
(3) $1101_2 \times 1001_2$
(4) $1111_2 \times 1111_2$

(5) $10101_2 \times 1100_2$
(6) $10011_2 \times 01100_2$
(7) $011001_2 \times 10000_2$
(8) $100110_2 \times 111_2$

7. Evaluate

(1) $1001.11_2 \times 100.101_2$
(2) $1100.011_2 \times 1.001_2$

(3) $10.0011_2 \times 111.01_2$
(4) $10011.111_2 \times 11101.001_2$

8. Evaluate

(1) $11001_2 \div 101_2$
(2) $1001000_2 \div 1001_2$
(3) $1011010_2 \div 110_2$

(4) $1101111_2 \div 10111_2$
(5) $101101_2 \div 111_2$
(6) $111111110_2 \div 11101_2$

9. (1) $1100.11_2 \div 11_2$
(2) $10011.1_2 \div 1101_2$

(3) $1000011.1_2 \div 101_2$
(4) $111111.11_2 \div 10001_2$

10. Carry out the following giving the answer to five binary places.

(1) $110011.1101_2 \div 1010_2$
(2) $1110001.0011_2 \div 1111_2$
(3) $100111001.0101_2 \div 10101_2$
(4) $110001011.00011_2 \div 11001_2$

Chapter 3

Negative numbers and computer arithmetic

3.1 Negative numbers in binary arithmetic

(1) The use of sign bits (the signed magnitude method)

The eight bit number 11111111_2 is equal to 255_{10}. Therefore eight bit numbers can vary from

$$00000000_2 \rightarrow 11111111_2 \text{ i.e. from } 0_{10} \rightarrow 255_{10}$$

Apart from the earlier mention in section 2.1 (subtraction) we have not considered the sign of the numbers we have used. This type of arithmetic, where the sign is not important, is called *un*signed arithmetic.

However, we are more often required to carry out processes where the signs of the numbers involved are important.

One method of doing this is to allow the most significant bit (that is the extreme left-hand digit) to represent the sign of the number. The figure 0 is considered to be positive and 1 to be negative. This is known as the signed magnitude method.

In this system the number

$$11111111_2 \text{ becomes} - (1111111)_2 = -127_{10}$$
$$\text{Similarly, } 01111111_2 \text{ becomes} - (1111111)_2 = +127_{10}$$

Therefore the unsigned range of numbers is decreased, i.e.

$0_{10} \rightarrow 127_{10}$, but the signed range of numbers is $-127_{10} \rightarrow +127_{10}$.

Using the method of sign bits (signed magnitude method) the number 0111_2 represents the binary number 111_2 with a positive sign in front of it. Thus the denary equivalent is given as

$$+ 1 \times 2^2 + 1 \times 2^1 + 1 \times 2^0 = + 7_{10}$$

In the same way 1111_2 is equal to -7_{10} since it is formed from a left-hand digit of 1 which is minus together with 111_2 which again gives 7_{10}.

There are disadvantages in the use of this method in computers and a more frequently adopted system is the *complement* system.

(2) The complement system

The idea of a complement has been considered in section 2.1. In this section we will consider it in much more detail and outline its use in computers.

There are two common types of complement which are of use in computer systems – the *one's complement* and the *two's complement*.

(a) One's complement

If a binary number has x digits and is subtracted from a number comprising x ones its one's complement is obtained, e.g. 1011001_2 has seven digits. The one's complement is obtained by subtracting it from the number containing seven ones, i.e. 1111111_2.

Thus:
$$
\begin{array}{r}
1111111 \\
1011001 \\
\hline
0100110 \\
\hline
\end{array}
$$

0100110_2 is the one's complement of 1011001_2.

The one's complement of 100_2 can be found in the same way

$$
\begin{array}{r}
111 \\
100 \\
\hline
011 \\
\hline
\end{array}
$$

Thus 011_2 is the one's complement of 100_2.

Note: If you look carefully at the above values you will see that the one's complement can also be obtained by inverting all of the digits of the original number.

(b) Two's complement

The two's complement is found by adding 1_2 to the one's complement. For example the two's complement of

(i) 1011001_2 is $0100110 + 1$ (ii) 100_2 is $011 + 1$
        $= 0100111_2$ $= 100_2$

Similarly that of 0111000_2 is $1000111 + 1 = 1001000_2$
and of 1000100_2 is $0111011 + 1 = 0111100_2$

Let us look at these numbers again closely

Number	101100	1	100	011	1000	1000	100
Complement	010011	1	100	100	1000	0111	100

In each case if we move from the extreme right until we reach the *first* one and leave everything to the *right* untouched but invert everything to the left we obtain the two's complement, e.g.:

Number	11001	100	101	10	10	100000
Two's complement	00110	100	010	10	01	100000

An important aspect of the two's complement number is that the most significant bit is used as a sign digit with 0 indicating a positive and 1 a negative quantity. Therefore from our above examples we see that the two's complements are described in denary numbers as follows:

01010_2 is $+ 0 \times 2^4 + 1 \times 2^3 + 0 \times 2^2 + 1 \times 2^1 + 0 \times 2^0 = 8 + 2 = 10_{10}$
1001000_2 is $- 1 \times 2^6 + 0 \times 2^5 + 0 \times 2^4 + 1 \times 2^3 + 0 \times 2^2 + 0 \times 2^1 + 0 \times 2^0$
$$= -64 + 8 = -56_{10}.$$

Now 01010_2 is the two's complement of 10110_2
and 10110_2 is $-1 \times 2^4 + 0 \times 2^3 + 1 \times 2^2 + 1 \times 2^1 + 0 \times 2^0$
$$= -16 + 4 + 2 = -10_{10}$$

$\therefore$ The two's complement of a number is equal in magnitude but opposite in sign to the original number.

0111000_2 is $0 \times 2^6 + 1 \times 2^5 + 1 \times 2^4 + 1 \times 2^3 + 0 \times 2^2 + 0 \times 2^1 + 0 \times 2^0$
$$= 32 + 16 + 8 = + 56_{10}$$

and the two's complement is seen from above to be -56_{10} supporting the rule.

Worked examples 3.1

Example 1. Use the signed magnitude method to convert (a) 0110_2 and (b) 1100101_2 to denary numbers.

(a) 0110_2 is $+ (1 \times 2^2 + 1 \times 2^1 + 0 \times 2^0) = + 4 + 2 = 6_{10}$
(b) 1100101_2 is $- (1 \times 2^5 + 0 \times 2^4 + 0 \times 2^3 + 1 \times 2^2 + 0 \times 2^1 + 1 \times 2^0)$
$$= -(32 + 4 + 1) = -37_{10}.$$

Example 2. Determine the two's complement of (a) 101011000_2 and (b) 0100100_2.

(a) Using one's complement

One's complement of 101011000_2 is 010100111_2
Two's complement is $010100111 + 1 = 01010 \quad 1000_2$

Check   original number is $10101 \quad 1000_2$

Therefore 010101000_2 is the two's complement of 101011000

(b) One's complement of 0100100_2 is $1011 \quad 011_2$
Two's complement is $1011011 + 1 = \quad 1011 \quad 100_2$

Check   original number is $0100 \quad 100_2$

Therefore 1011100_2 is the two's complement of 0100100_2

3.2 Computer arithmetic

One of the problems concerned with the application of digital computers is that not only have they got to be used in the binary system but they are usually only capable of carrying out the process of addition. Therefore in some way the processes of subtraction, multiplication and division must be converted to addition.

(1) Subtraction

This is achieved by the use of the two's complement. For example, subtract 10010_2 from 11100_2.
The two's complement of 10010 is 01110.
Add this to the minuend 11100

```
 11100
 01110
```
$\overline{101010}$

Now ignore the most significant bit to give 01010_2.

By subtraction:

11100	28
10010	18
01010	10

The method is:

(i) find the two's complement of the subtrahend;
(ii) add this to the minuend;
(iii) ignore the carry bit at the extreme left of the answer.

Alternatively, we can use the one's complement as follows:

(i) find the one's complement of the subtrahend. In the above case this is 01101;
(ii) add the complement to the minuend:

```
   11100
   01101
  ──────
[1] 01001
  └──────→1        see section 2.1
  ──────
   01010
  ──────
```

In both addition methods there is an extra digit produced. This denotes a positive answer. If there is no digit the answer is negative.

(2) Multiplication

This is done by the shift and add method. For example, multiply 11011_2 by 1100111_2.

11011	11011×1	11011
1100111	shift one to left $\times 1$	11011
11011		1010001
11011	shift one to left $\times 1$	11011
1010001	shift two to left (two 0's)	10111101
11011	shift one to left $\times 1$	11011**
10111101		10000011101
11011**	shift one to left $\times 1$	11011
10000011101		101011011101
11011		
101011011101		

Check by denary multiplication $27_{10} \times 103_{10} = 2781_{10}$.

It can be seen from the above that multiplication is carried out by a process of repeated addition. Note that in each case the presence of a zero in the multiplier is allowed for by moving one place to the left for each zero.

(3) Division

The normal process of division is not possible since unlike multiplication this involves subtraction rather than addition. However, we have seen under (1) that subtraction can be replaced by addition.

Let us consider how we may use addition in the process of division by dividing 11100_2 by 100_2.

The two's complement of $100 = 011 + 1 = 100$.

In normal division we subtract the divisor whilst in computer calculations we add the two's complement. *In this example note that the divisor and the two's complement are the same.*

(a) Division by subtraction   (b) Division by adding two's
                                    complement

```
        111
100 | 111000                                11100
      100 –                                  100 +
      ───                                    ─────
       110            delete carry          10110      1
       100 –                                 100 +
       ───                                   ─────
        100           delete carry           10100     1
        100 –                                 100 +
        ───                                   ─────
        000           delete carry            1000     1
        ───                                    ─────
```

In both cases we obtain an answer of 111_2 and no remainder. Let us now look at a more complex example:

10000010_2 divided by 1010_2

Using method (b) the two's complement of 1010 is 0110

```
10000010
0110 +
────────
1110
```

Now since the left-hand digit is one and is *not* a carry digit the answer is negative. If we look at the example by division.

```
         0
1010 | 10000010
```

The first number in the quotient is 0 since 1010 does not divide into 1000, i.e. 1000 – 1010 is negative.

We can now look at the addition method again

```
 ┌─► 10000010
 │    0110
 │   ─────
 │    1110        negative therefore     0
 └─► 10000
      0110
     ─────
     X01100       carry one              1
      0110
     ─────
 ┌─► X00101       carry one              1
 │    0110
 │   ─────
 │    1011        negative therefore     0
 └─► 001010
      0110
     ─────
     X0000        carry one              1
```

If we carry out the division in the normal way we obtain:

```
            01101
      ┌──────────
1010  │  10000010
         1010
        ──────
         01100
         1010
        ──────
         001010
          1010
         ──────
          0000
```

In both cases the answer is 1101 with no remainder.

In all of the above cases we have subtraction, multiplication and division replaced by addition plus other steps (e.g. shifting of points, deletion of lines followed by return to the previous stage) which are capable of being carried out by a computer.

Worked example 3.2

Example 1. Solve the following using suitable addition methods.

(a) $1110111_2 - 0100011_2$ (b) $11001_2 \times 11001101_2$ (c) $1110010 \div 110_2$

Answer

(a) (i) One's complement: The one's complement of 0100011_2 is 1011100_2

```
  1110111                        119
  1011100 +                       35 –
```
[1] 1010011
     └──→ 1
```
 ⁰1010100  84                      84
```

(ii) Two's complement: The two's complement of 0100011_2 is 1011101_2

```
    1110111
    1011101
```
ɫ 1010100   delete extra carry.

The extra digit in (i) and (ii) denotes a positive answer.

(b) $11001_2 \times 11001101_2$

	11001	25
2 steps to left × 1	11001	205
	1111101	125
1 step to left × 1	11001	50
	101000101	
3 steps to left × 1	11001	
	11110000101	
1 step to left × 1	11001	
	1010000000101	5125

(c) $1110010_2 \div 110_2$
The two's complement of 110_2 is 010_2

```
  1110010                              19
  010                              6 │ 114
 ┌─ ɫ0010      1                       6
 │  010                               54
 │  100        0                       54
 ├─ 00100                              00
 │  010
 │  110        0
 └→ 001001
    010
    ɫ0110      1
    010
    ɫ000       1
```

Thus $1110010_2 \div 110_2 = 10011_2$.

Example 2. Divide 10101111_2 by 1110_2 until there is no remainder.

Answer. The two's complement of 1110_2 is 0010_2.

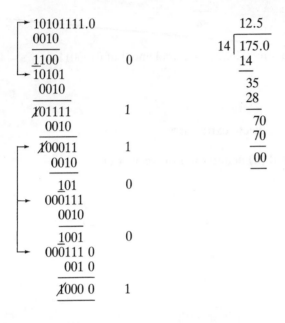

The answer is 01100.1_2.

Exercise 3

Section 3.1

1. Convert the following to denary numbers using the signed magnitude method:

(1) 11100_2 (6) 01010_2
(2) 01100_2 (7) 110101_2
(3) 0101_2 (8) 1011101_2
(4) 011001_2 (9) 111001_2
(5) 1001_2 (10) 010010_2

2. Determine the one's complement and the two's complement of the following binary numbers:

(1) 1101010   (4) 10010110
(2) 0110100   (5) 111101010
(3) 00111000   (6) 10100001

Section 3.2

3. Repeat questions 4 and 5 of Exercise 2 using the two's complement.

4. Repeat questions 6 and 7 of Exercise 2 using the add and shift method.

5. Repeat questions 8 and 9 of Exercise 2 using an addition method.

Chapter 4

Logic gates and truth tables

4.1 Introduction

In chapters 1, 2 and 3 we have been looking at the binary system of numbers and how it can be used to carry out the normal processes of arithmetic in much the same way as the more familiar denary system. The main reason for studying the binary system was because of its use in computer calculations.

In the remaining chapters of the book we will be considering the algebra of binary processes. This is usually called Boolean algebra after its inventor. The main reason for studying it is that it can enable us to simplify the very complex circuitry used in computers (see section 6.3). There is a close link between Boolean algebra and electrical circuits. A detailed examination of how switches combine in series and parallel in circuits to give an electrical output will help us to understand and use Boolean algebra more effectively. In addition, we often need to create an output where there is no input. The circuit element which provides the required output is known as a *logic gate*. The three basic gates and some modifications are considered in detail in section 4.3. In the circuits which follow we shall be considering mechanical switches only although in computer technology these are replaced by semiconductor devices.

We have defined the gates as logic gates and to understand why this is so we must look at what is meant by logic.

4.2 Logic

Logic is concerned with the truth or falseness of statements which are made by us and by others, whether written or spoken. For example, if the statement 'today is Friday' is true then the statements 'tomorrow is Saturday' and 'yesterday was Thursday' are also true. In the same way if 'today is Friday' the statement 'yesterday was Wednesday' is false. The truth or otherwise of the last three statements follows as a logical consequence from the truth of the first. Note that each of the above statements is either true *or* false. None can be both true *and* false.

Since there are only two possible conditions to any logic statement (true or false), logic is a two-state system.

Let us now examine the sentence 'When the light is switched on in the bathroom the bathroom vent starts to work.' There are two statements contained in this sentence:

the light is switched on in the bathroom

the bathroom vent starts to work

The second statement is a logical consequence of the first, i.e. if the first happens so does the second but not otherwise. In computer technology the situation is more complex and we usually need a number of switches in a given combination to give the appropriate output. The resulting combination of switches is a gate. Since the output follows as a logical consequence of the input to the gate, the gate is called a logic gate. As stated in section 4.1 there are three basic gates and these will now be discussed in turn.

4.3 Logic gates

(1) The AND gate

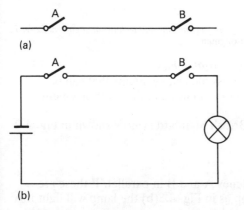

Fig. 4.1 *Source: Computer technology for technicians and technician engineers Level 1, by R. V. Watkin (1976), Longman.*

38

Figure 4.1(a) shows two switches A and B in series. If these are placed in a circuit with a lamp as in Fig. 4.1(b), the lamp will light if, and only if, switch A *and* switch B are closed. In all other circumstances the lamp will remain off.

This is shown clearly in Table 4.1.

It was defined earlier (section 1.1) that an open switch has a value 0 and a closed switch a value 1. Therefore an alternative form of Table 4.1 can be constructed (Table 4.2).

Table 4.1

Switch A	Switch B	Lamp
open	open	off
open	closed	off
closed	open	off
closed	closed	on

Table 4.2

Switch A	Switch B	Lamp
0	0	0
0	1	0
1	0	0
1	1	1

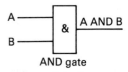

AND gate

Fig. 4.2 *Source: Computer technology for technicians and technician engineers Level 1, by R. V. Watkin (1976), Longman.*

Tables of this kind are known as *truth tables*.

Truth tables show all the possible arrangements that can be obtained for any combination of switches and those arrangements which give rise to an output.

The AND gate has the British Standard symbol shown in Fig. 4.2.

(2) The OR gate

Figure 4.3(a) shows two switches A and B in parallel. If these are placed in a circuit with a lamp as in Fig. 4.3(b) the lamp will light if A *or* B *or* both A and B are closed.

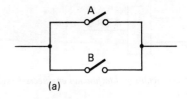

(a)

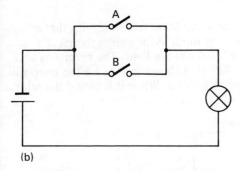

(b)

Fig. 4.3 *Source: Computer technology for technicians and technician engineers Level 1, by R. V. Watkin (1976), Longman.*

The truth tables representing the OR gate and the so-called OR function are given in Tables 4.3 and 4.4

Table 4.3

Switch A	Switch B	Lamp
open	open	off
open	closed	on
closed	open	on
closed	closed	on

Table 4.4

Switch A	Switch B	Lamp
0	0	0
0	1	1
1	0	1
1	1	1

The British Standard symbol for the OR gate is shown in Fig. 4.4. The symbol on the right is more accurate but is not necessary in the context of this book.

40

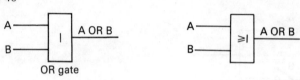

Fig. 4.4 *Source: Computer technology for technicians and technician engineers Level 1, by R. V. Watkin (1976), Longman.*

(3) The NOT gate

Sometimes it is useful to produce a condition which negates that of the switch. In other words if there is an input at the switch there is no output from the circuit and the lamp will not light. The reverse is also true. For a simple relay circuit like that shown in Fig. 4.5 the lamp will remain alight as long as the switch is open. When it is closed the relay switch will open and the light will go out.

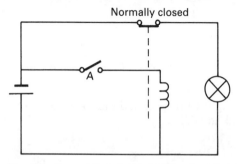

Fig. 4.5 *Source: Computer technology for technicians and technician engineers Level 1, by R. V. Watkin (1976), Longman.*

The appropriate truth tables are given in Tables 4.5 and 4.6. The symbol for the NOT gate is given in Fig. 4.6. Again the symbol on the right is more accurate.

Table 4.5

Switch A	Lamp
open	on
closed	off

Table 4.6

Switch A	Lamp
0	1
1	0

In addition to the simple gates considered above there are two combination gates which need to be dealt with in detail.

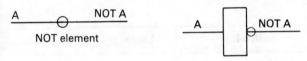

NOT element

Fig. 4.6 *Source: Computer technology for technicians and technician engineers Level 1*, by R. V. Watkin (1976), Longman.

(4) The NAND (or NOT AND) gate

This is an AND gate in a circuit in combination with a NOT gate which inverts the output from the AND gate. This is reflected in the truth tables (Tables 4.7 and 4.8) which should be compared with Tables 4.1 and 4.2.

Table 4.7

Switch A	Switch B	Lamp
open	open	on
open	closed	on
closed	open	on
closed	closed	off

Table 4.8

Switch A	Switch B	Lamp
0	0	1
0	1	1
1	0	1
1	1	0

The combination of symbols for the NAND gate is given in Fig. 4.7.

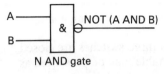

N AND gate

Fig. 4.7 *Source: Computer technology for technicians and technician engineers Level 1*, by R. V. Watkin (1976) Longman.

(5) The NOR (or NOT OR) gate

As in the previous case the combination of the NOT and OR gates in a circuit will produce the inverse of the OR gate.

The truth tables are shown in Tables 4.9 and 4.10 (compare with Tables 4.3 and 4.4).

Table 4.9

Switch A	Switch B	Lamp
open	open	on
open	closed	off
closed	open	off
closed	closed	off

Table 4.10

Switch A	Switch B	Lamp
0	0	1
0	1	0
1	0	0
1	1	0

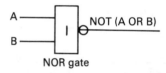

NOR gate

Fig. 4.8 *Source: Computer technology for technicians and technician engineers Level 1, by R. V. Watkin (1976), Longman.*

The combination of symbols for the NOR gate is given in Fig. 4.8.

Examples of the design and construction of more complex circuits containing three switches are given below. Integrated circuit manufacturers use international (MIL) symbols as shown in the Appendix on page 78.

Worked examples 4.2

Example 1. Construct a truth table for a circuit containing a lamp with three switches A, B, C in series.
Answer Since the lamp will work only if all three switches are closed (this is a three-input AND gate), the truth table may be presented as shown in Tables 4.11 and 4.12.

Example 2 Construct a truth table for a circuit containing three switches A, B, C in parallel with a lamp in the circuit.
Answer This is a three-input OR gate and will have an output as long as any one or more of the switches is closed. The truth tables are shown in Tables 4.13 and 4.14.

Table 4.11

	Switch A	Switch B	Switch C	Lamp
All switches open	open	open	open	off
One switch closed	open	open	closed	off
	open	closed	open	off
	closed	open	open	off
Two switches closed	open	closed	closed	off
	closed	open	closed	off
	closed	closed	open	off
All switches closed	closed	closed	closed	on

Table 4.12

Switch A	Switch B	Switch C	Lamp
0	0	0	0
0	0	1	0
0	1	0	0
1	0	0	0
0	1	1	0
1	0	1	0
1	1	0	0
1	1	1	1

Table 4.13

Switch A	Switch B	Switch C	Lamp
open	open	open	off
open	open	closed	on
open	closed	open	on
closed	open	open	on
open	closed	closed	on
closed	open	closed	on
closed	closed	open	on
closed	closed	closed	on

Table 4.14

Switch A	Switch B	Switch C	Lamp
0	0	0	0
0	0	1	1
0	1	0	1
1	0	0	1
0	1	1	1
1	0	1	1
1	1	0	1
1	1	1	1

Example 3 A circuit consists of a lamp and three switches A, B and C as shown in Fig. 4.9. Under what conditions will the lamp light? Draw a truth table of the results. Draw the resulting logic gate in symbol form.

Answer Since A is in series with the other two switches the light will not go on when A is open. However, when A is closed and either B *or* C *or* B and C is closed the lamp will light. The truth tables are shown in Tables 4.15 and 4.16.

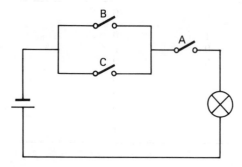

Fig. 4.9

Table 4.15

Switch A	Switch B	Switch C	Lamp
open	open	open	off
open	open	closed	off
open	closed	open	off
open	closed	closed	off
closed	open	open	off
closed	open	closed	on
closed	closed	open	on
closed	closed	closed	on

Table 4.16

Switch A	Switch B	Switch C	Lamp
0	0	0	0
0	0	1	0
0	1	0	0
0	1	1	0
1	0	0	0
1	0	1	1
1	1	0	1
1	1	1	1

The resulting logic gate is shown in symbol form in Fig. 4.10.
Other applications will be considered in chapter 5.

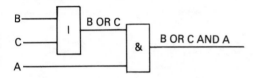

Fig. 4.10

Exercise 4

Section 4.3

1. Construct truth tables for the following combinations of gates

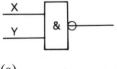

(a)

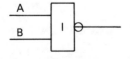

(b)

46

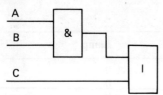

(c)

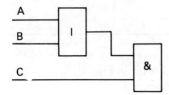

(d)

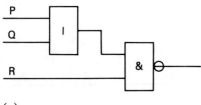

(e)

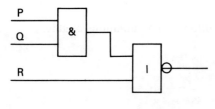

(f)

Chapter 5

Boolean algebra

5.1 Introduction

In the first three chapters of the book we were mainly concerned with
the arithmetical aspects of binary processes. In this and the final
chapter we will be looking at the algebra involved in two-state
processes and some of its applications to switch devices. It is known as
Boolean algebra after the inventor Charles Boole. In common with
other forms of algebra one important use of Boolean algebra is in the
simplification of algebraic statements. This is important in computer
technology, for example, in the simplification of complex switching
devices.

　　The laws of Boolean algebra will be developed in relation to the
two-state processes, logic and switching circuitry.

5.2 Logic processes

In logic a statement which is true *or* false but not true *and* false is
called a *proposition*. If two or more propositions are joined together
the result is called a *compound proposition*. Let us consider the
sentence 'A pump will work when the electricity is switched on, when
the water in the boiler is hot and when the oil pressure is high enough.'
If the three propositions
　　the electricity is switched on

the water in the boiler is hot
the oil pressure is high enough
are all true the resulting proposition
the pump will work
is also true.

Let us examine some simple compound propositions more deeply.

(i) The alarm bell is switched on when the back door is opened and/or the front door is opened.

Let a represent the proposition 'the back door is opened'
Let b represent the proposition 'the front door is opened'
Let z represent the resulting proposition 'the alarm bell is switched on'

If a and b are true OR if a is true OR if b is true, z is true, i.e. if a **and/or** b is true z is true.

The statement
the back door is opened and/or the front door is opened
is represented by $a + b$
$\therefore$ $z = a + b$
z is called the *disjunction* of two propositions where a **and/or** b is true.

(ii) The bank vault is opened by using both the manager's key and the assistant manager's key but not otherwise.

Let a represent 'the manager's key is used'
Let b represent 'the assistant manager's key is used'

If, and only if, a **and** b is true, is z true.

The statement
the manager's key **and** the assistant manager's key is used but not otherwise
is represented by $a \cdot b$
$\therefore z = a \cdot b$
z is called the *conjunction* of two propositions when a **and** b is true.

(iii) Let us consider the propositions 'the window is open' and 'the window is shut'.
Clearly if the first proposition is true then the second one is false and vice versa.

If 'the window is open' is represented by a
then 'the window is shut' is represented by $\bar{a}$

Thus we have *negation* of the first proposition by the second. The horizontal line above a letter representing a statement always signifies a negation of that statement.

It can be seen from (i), (ii) and (iii) that:
 (i) if two statements are joined by 'and/or' the symbols representing the statements are joined by '+';
(ii) if two statements are joined by 'and' the symbols representing the statements are joined by '·';
(iii) if one statement is true the negation of that statement is given by a bar over the symbol representing the statement.

We can determine whether a compound proposition is true or false by the use of truth tables (see Examples 5.2, 3 and 4).

Worked examples 5.2

Example 1. A conveyor belt moves forward when a photoelectric cell (C_1) receives light and or a photoelectric cell (C_2) does not receive light. Express this statement in suitable algebraic form.

Answer

Let z represent	'the belt moves forward'
a represent	'the photoelectric cell (C_1) receives light'
b represent	'the photoelectric cell (C_2) receives light'
therefore $\bar{b}$ represents	'the photoelectric cell (C_2) does not receive light'

Expressed in algebraic form $z = a + \bar{b}$

Example 2. The interior light in a car goes out only when both the nearside and the offside doors are closed. Express this statement in suitable algebraic form.

Answer

Let z represent	'the interior light in a car goes out'
a represent	'the nearside door is closed'
b represent	'the offside door is closed'

Expressed in Boolean form $z = a \cdot b$

Example 3 By the use of a truth table show that

$$(a + b) \cdot (a + b) = a + b.$$

Answer A truth table consisting of a, b, $a + b$ and $(a + b) \cdot (a + b)$ is constructed as shown in Table 5.1.

It can be seen from the table that the columns $a + b$ and $(a + b) \cdot (a + b)$ are identical. Therefore

$$(a + b) \cdot (a + b) = a + b$$

Table 5.1

a	b	$a + b$	$(a + b) \cdot (a + b)$
0	0	0	0
0	1	1	1
1	0	1	1
1	1	1	1

Example 4 Using a truth table show that

$$a \cdot b \cdot c = \bar{a} + \bar{b} + \bar{c}$$

Answer Construct a table containing a, b, c, $\bar{a}$, $\bar{b}$, $\bar{c}$, $\bar{a} + \bar{b} + \bar{c}$, $a \cdot b \cdot c$ and $\overline{a \cdot b \cdot c}$ as shown in Table 5.2.

It can be seen from Table 5.2 that the values under $\bar{a} + \bar{b} + \bar{c}$ and $a \cdot b \cdot c$ are the same. Therefore

$$\overline{a \cdot b \cdot c} = \bar{a} + \bar{b} + \bar{c}$$

Table 5.2

a	b	c	$\bar{a}$	$\bar{b}$	$\bar{c}$	$\bar{a} + \bar{b} + \bar{c}$	$a \cdot b \cdot c$	$\overline{a \cdot b \cdot c}$
0	0	0	1	1	1	1	0	1
0	0	1	1	1	0	1	0	1
0	1	0	1	0	1	1	0	1
1	0	0	0	1	1	1	0	1
0	1	1	1	0	0	1	0	1
1	0	1	0	1	0	1	0	1
1	1	0	0	0	1	1	0	1
1	1	1	0	0	0	0	1	0

5.3 Switch circuits

Since switches are two-state devices they can be treated in the same way as logic propositions.

(1) Switches in parallel (OR situation)

If two switches in parallel are connected in a circuit with a lamp (Fig. 4.3), the lamp will light when either or both of the switches are depressed. Let the switches be A and B and the resulting combination be Z.

The lamp will light when A **and** B are on, OR when A is on, OR when B is on, i.e. the lamp will light when A **and/or** B is on.

$\therefore Z = A + B$ (section 5.2 (i))

(2) Switches in series (AND situation)

If two switches in series are connected in a circuit with a lamp (Fig. 4.1) the lamp will light if, and only if, both switches are depressed. Let the switches be A and B and the resulting combination be Z.

The lamp will light when, and only when, A **and** B are on.

$\therefore Z = A \cdot B$ (section 5.2(ii))

(3) NOT situation

Let A be the switch in the circuit such that when it is on, the light is off and when it is off the light is on (Fig. 4.5). Let Z be the result.

In this case $Z = \bar{A}$ (section 5.2 (iii))

Worked examples 5.3

Example 1   Write down a Boolean expression for the combinations of gates given in (i) Fig. 5.1 and (ii) Fig. 5.2.

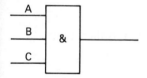

Fig. 5.1

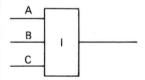

Fig. 5.2

Answer (i) The gate represents three switches in series and is therefore represented by

     $A \cdot B \cdot C$

 (ii) The gate represents three switches in parallel and is therefore represented by

     $A + B + C$

Example 2 Write down a Boolean expression for the combinations of gates shown in Figs. 5.3 and 5.4.

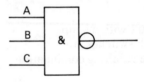

Fig. 5.3

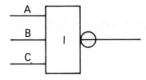

Fig. 5.4

Answer Figure 5.3 is Fig. 5.1 with a NOT gate added and it is therefore represented by

$\overline{A \cdot B \cdot C}$

Figure 5.4 is Fig. 5.2 with a NOT gate added and it is therefore represented by

$\overline{A + B + C}$

Example 3 Write down a Boolean expression for the gate combination shown in Fig. 5.5.

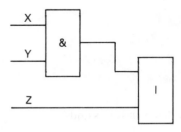

Fig. 5.5

Answer In Fig. 5.5 X and Y form an AND gate to give
X·Y
This is then combined with Z in an OR gate to give
(X·Y) + Z

Exercise 5

Section 5.2

Express the following statements in suitable algebraic form:

1. When either the front nearside door or the front offside door is opened in a car, the interior light comes on.
2. Addition of a given reagent forms an orange precipitate when either sodium or potassium is present in a mixture.
3. A safety device is provided for a machine so that when the switch is on and the safety device is on, and only in this case, will the machine work.
4. A conveyor belt carrying empty jars passes over a light. When a jar stops and light passes through the jar then liquid will fall from a reservoir above.

Using truth tables prove that the left-hand side of the equations in each of the following examples is equal to the right-hand side:

5. $a + \bar{a} \cdot b \cdot c + \bar{a} \cdot b \cdot \bar{c} = a + b$
6. $a + a \cdot b = a$
7. $(a + b) \cdot (a + \bar{b} + \bar{c}) = a + b \cdot \bar{c}$
8. $(a + b) \cdot (b + c) \cdot (c + a) = a \cdot b + a \cdot c + b \cdot c$
9. Write down Boolean expressions for the combinations of gates in Exercise 4.

Chapter 6

Rules and application of Boolean algebra to switching circuits

6.1 Switch circuits and the rules of Boolean algebra

The techniques used in the previous chapter can be applied to switch circuits and we have already seen that:

$z = a + b$ as applied to logic relates to the OR function. Hence $Z = A + B$

$z = a \cdot b$ as applied to logic relates to the AND function. Hence $Z = A \cdot B$

Negation as applied to logic relates to the NOT function. Hence $Z = \overline{A}$

Note that we use small letters for logic statements and capitals for switches, z normally representing a compound proposition and Z the final gate or combination of gates.

As in other branches of algebra, certain laws can be shown to hold for Boolean algebra.

(1) Commutative laws

As in normal algebra the order in which A and B are taken in addition and multiplication (but not in subtraction) does not affect the result, i.e.:

$A + B$	$= B + A$	(Rule 1)
and $A \cdot B$	$= B \cdot A$	(Rule 2)

These results can be confirmed by the use of truth tables as shown in worked examples 5.2. The appropriate truth tables can be seen in Tables 6.1 and 6.2.

It is clearly seen from Table 6.1 that Rule 1 is obeyed and from Table 6.2 that Rule 2 is obeyed.

Table 6.1

A	B	A + B	B + A
0	0	0	0
0	1	1	1
1	0	1	1
1	1	1	1

Table 6.2

A	B	A·B	B·A
0	0	0	0
0	1	0	0
1	0	0	0
1	1	1	1

(2) Associative laws

The order in which three switches are taken when adding or multiplying does not affect the result. For three switches A, B and C

$$A + B + C = (A + B) + C = A + (B + C) \qquad \text{Rule 3}$$
$$A \cdot B \cdot C \quad = (A \cdot B) \cdot C = A \cdot (B \cdot C) \qquad \text{Rule 4}$$

Again these results can be confirmed by the use of truth tables (Tables 6.3 and 6.4).
It can be seen from Table 6.3 that Rule 3 is obeyed and from Table 6.4 that Rule 4 is obeyed.

Table 6.3

A	B	C	A + B	B + C	A + B + C	A + (B + C)	(A + B) + C
0	0	0	0	0	0	0	0
0	0	1	0	1	1	1	1
0	1	0	1	1	1	1	1
1	0	0	1	0	1	1	1
0	1	1	1	1	1	1	1
1	0	1	1	1	1	1	1
1	1	0	1	1	1	1	1
1	1	1	1	1	1	1	1

Table 6.4

A	B	C	A·B	B·C	A·B·C	A·(B·C)	(A·B)·C
0	0	0	0	0	0	0	0
0	0	1	0	0	0	0	0
0	1	0	0	0	0	0	0
1	0	0	0	0	0	0	0
0	1	1	0	1	0	0	0
1	0	1	0	0	0	0	0
1	1	0	1	0	0	0	0
1	1	1	1	1	1	1	1

(3) Distributive laws

$$A \cdot (B + C) = A \cdot B + A \cdot C \qquad\qquad \text{Rule 5}$$
$$A + B \cdot C = (A + B) \cdot (A + C) \qquad\qquad \text{Rule 6}$$

Although it can be seen that Rule 5 has its counterpart in normal algebra it is clear that this is not true of Rule 6. Once again these results can be confirmed by truth tables (Tables 6.5 and 6.6).

Table 6.5

A	B	C	B + C	A·B	A·C	A·(B + C)	A·B + A·C
0	0	0	0	0	0	0	0
0	0	1	1	0	0	0	0
0	1	0	1	0	0	0	0
1	0	0	0	0	0	0	0
0	1	1	1	0	0	0	0
1	0	1	1	0	1	1	1
1	1	0	1	1	0	1	1
1	1	1	1	1	1	1	1

Table 6.6

A	B	C	B·C	A + B	A + C	(A + B)·(A + C)	A + B·C
0	0	0	0	0	0	0	0
0	0	1	0	0	1	0	0
0	1	0	0	1	0	0	0
1	0	0	0	1	1	1	1
0	1	1	1	1	1	1	1
1	0	1	0	1	1	1	1
1	1	0	0	1	1	1	1
1	1	1	1	1	1	1	1

Again it can be seen from Table 6.5 that Rule 5 is obeyed and from Table 6.6 that Rule 6 is obeyed.

In addition to the above laws there are a number of useful identities which should be remembered. These are based on OR and AND functions.

(4)   Identities based on OR functions

A   B   Z

(1) $A + 1 = 1$ Since one of the switches is always on, current will always flow, $Z = 1$.
(2) $A + 0 = A$ If $A = 0$ no current flows, $Z = 0$; If $A = 1$ current flows, $Z = 1$.
(3) $A + A = A$ If $A = 0$ no current flows, $Z = 0$; If $A = 1$ current flows, $Z = 1$.
(4) $A + \bar{A} = 1$ If $A = 0$, $\bar{A} = 1$ and current flows, $Z = 1$; If $A = 1$, $\bar{A} = 0$ and current flows, $Z = 1$.

In cases (2) and (3) Z always has the same value as A. Therefore $Z = A$.

(5)   Identities based on AND functions

A   B   Z

(5) $A \cdot 1 = A$ If $A = 0$ no current flows, $Z = 0$; If $A = 1$ current flows, $Z = 1$.
(6) $A \cdot 0 = 0$ Since $B = 0$ no current can flow, $Z = 0$.
(7) $A \cdot A = A$ If $A = 0$ no current flows, $Z = 0$; If $A = 1$ **both** switches are on, current flows, $Z = 1$.
(8) $A \cdot \bar{A} = 0$ If $A = 1$, $\bar{A} = 0$ and if $A = 0$, $\bar{A} = 1$. In both cases one switch is off, no current flows, $Z = 0$.

In cases (5) and (7) Z always has the same value as A. Therefore $Z = A$.

(6)   Identities based on the NOT function

Two identities (4) and (8) have already been discussed. There is one other.

(9) $\bar{\bar{A}} = A$

$\bar{\bar{A}}$ represents the negation of the negation of A, i.e.:

If A is on, $\bar{A}$ is off and $\bar{\bar{A}}$ is on.
If A is off $\bar{A}$ is on and $\bar{\bar{A}}$ is off.

This confirms identity number (9).

Table 6.7

$A + B = B + A$	(1)
$A + 1 = 1$	(2)
$A + 0 = 0$	(3)
$A + A = A$	(4)
$A + \bar{A} = 1$	(5)
$A \cdot B = B \cdot A$	(6)
$A \cdot 1 = A$	(7)
$A \cdot 0 = 0$	(8)
$A \cdot A = A$	(9)
$A \cdot \bar{A} = 0$	(10)
$\bar{\bar{A}} = A$	(11)
$A + B + C = (A + B) + C = A + (B + C)$	(12)
$A \cdot B \cdot C = (A \cdot B) \cdot C = A \cdot (B \cdot C)$	(13)
$A \cdot (B + C) = A \cdot B + A \cdot C$	(14)
$A + B \cdot C = (A + B) \cdot (A + C)$	(15)

6.2 Derivation of Boolean expressions

In this section we will be mainly concerned with the construction of Boolean expressions from switching circuits, from logic networks and from truth tables and the techniques will be exemplified by means of worked examples.

Worked examples 6.2

Example 1. From the switching system shown in Fig. 6.1 construct a suitable logic network and Boolean equation to express it.

Answer. It may be seen from Fig. 6.1 that there are two branches of the system in parallel.

One branch consists of two switches in parallel with each other and in series with a third.

The second branch consists of two switches in series.

In the first branch A and B form an OR gate to give $A + B$. This will then join with C in an AND gate to give $(A + B) \cdot C$.

In the second branch A and B will form an AND gate to give $A \cdot B$.

These will both form an OR gate to give the Boolean expression

$(A + B) \cdot C + A \cdot B$

In order for there to be an output for the system the Boolean expression must be equal to 1.

Hence the resulting Boolean equation is

$(A + B) \cdot C + A \cdot B = 1$

The logic network for this system is given in Fig. 6.2.

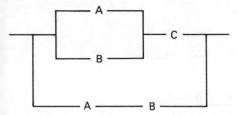

Fig. 6.1

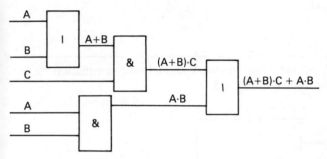

Fig. 6.2

Example 2 Construct a logic network and a Boolean expression for the switching system shown in Fig. 6.3.

Answer. The system contains three branches in parallel.

In the first branch A and B are in series and will form an AND gate to give $A \cdot B$.

In the second branch C, D, E are in series and will form an AND gate to give $C \cdot D \cdot E$.

These are in parallel with C in the third branch and will form an OR gate to give the Boolean expression

$A \cdot B + C \cdot D \cdot E + C$

The logic network is given in Fig. 6.4.

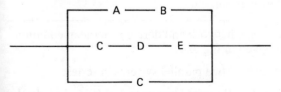

Fig. 6.3

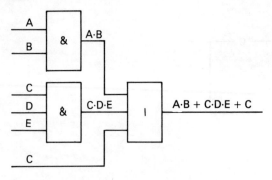

Fig. 6.4

Example 3 Construct a logic network and a Boolean equation for the switching system shown in Fig. 6.5.

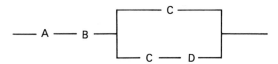

Fig. 6.5

Answer. The system contains two switches in series with a parallel system. In the parallel portion, the switches C and D will form an AND gate to give C·D which with C will then form an OR gate to give

C·D + C

The first two switches A and B will form an AND gate to give A·B then form a second AND gate with (C·D + C) to give the Boolean expression

A·B·(C·D + C)

The related Boolean equation is

A·B (C·D + C) = 1

The logic network is shown in Fig. 6.6

Example 4 Construct a logic network and derive a Boolean equation for the switching circuit given in Fig. 6.7.

Answer. The circuit consists of two parallel systems in series:

(i) In the first parallel system there are two branches (Fig. 6.8). In the first branch A forms a NOT gate to give $\overline{A}$ and then with B in series forms an AND gate to give $\overline{A}$·B.

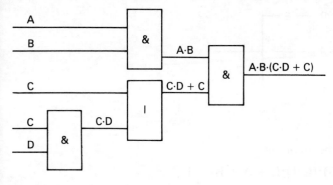

Fig. 6.6

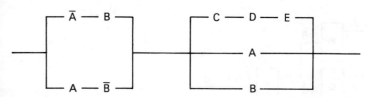

Fig. 6.7

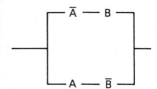

Fig. 6.8

In the second branch B forms a NOT gate to give $\overline{B}$ and then with A in series forms an AND gate to give $A \cdot B$.

$\overline{A} \cdot B$ and $A \cdot \overline{B}$ then form an OR gate to give

$$\overline{A} \cdot B + A \cdot \overline{B}$$

(ii) In the second parallel system there are three branches (Fig. 6.9).

In the first C, D and E form an AND gate to give $C \cdot D \cdot E$ which together with A and B in parallel with it form an OR gate to give

$$C \cdot D \cdot E + A + B$$

The resultants from (i) and (ii), since they are in series, finally form an AND gate to give

$$(\overline{A} \cdot B + A \cdot \overline{B}) \cdot (C \cdot D \cdot E + A + B)$$

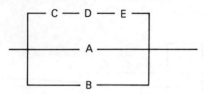

Fig. 6.9

For there to be an output
$$(\overline{A}\cdot B + A\cdot\overline{B})\cdot(C\cdot D\cdot E + A + B) = 1$$
The logic network is given in Fig. 6.10.

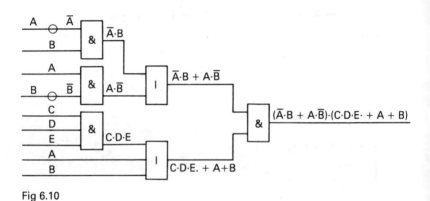

Fig 6.10

Example 5 From the truth table (Table 6.8) derive the related Boolean equation, and draw a diagram of the resultant switching system.

Table 6.8

	A	B	Z
(1)	0	0	1
(2)	0	1	0
(3)	1	0	1
(4)	1	1	0

Answer. For there to be an output from a circuit Z must equal 1. This is true in lines (1) and (3).

Line (1) Both A and B are zero, therefore $\bar{A}$ and $\bar{B}$ are one.
Hence $\bar{A} = \bar{B} = 1$
Line (3) B is zero, therefore $\bar{B}$ is one.
Hence $A = \bar{B} = 1$

Therefore the Boolean equation is

$$\bar{A} \cdot \bar{B} + A \cdot \bar{B} = 1$$

The circuit for the truth table is shown in Fig. 6.11.

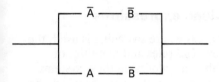

Fig. 6.11

Example 6 From the truth table (Table 6.9) derive the related Boolean equation and construct a switching circuit which obeys that equation.

Table 6.9

	A	B	C	Z
(1)	0	0	0	0
(2)	0	0	1	0
(3)	0	1	0	1
(4)	1	0	0	1
(5)	0	1	1	1
(6)	1	0	1	0
(7)	1	1	0	0
(8)	1	1	1	1

Answer In lines (3), (4), (5) and (8) $Z = 1$
Hence in line (3) $\bar{A} = B = \bar{C} = 1$
(4) $A = \bar{B} = \bar{C} = 1$
(5) $\bar{A} = B = C = 1$
(8) $A = B = C = 1$

Therefore the resultant Boolean equation is

$$\bar{A} \cdot B \cdot \bar{C} + A \cdot \bar{B} \cdot \bar{C} + \bar{A} \cdot B \cdot C + A \cdot B \cdot C = 1$$

The circuit for the truth table is shown in Fig. 6.12.

64

Fig. 6.12

6.3 Simplification of Boolean expressions

In computer technology and other areas where switching is used, the systems are frequently very complex. The rules and identities of Boolean algebra can often be valuable in simplifying these systems, mainly to allow for decreases in cost. Some of the ways by which this can be achieved are considered in this section by means of worked examples. The examples considered are simpler than those normally encountered in practice but the methods employed are the same. Truth tables can be used to ensure that the simplifications are justifiable.

Worked examples 6.3

Example 1 Simplify the following Boolean expressions and confirm the answer by using truth tables: (a) $\bar{A} \cdot \bar{B} + A \cdot \bar{B}$ (see example 6.2.5); (b) $A \cdot B + A \cdot \bar{B}$; (c) $A \cdot B + A \cdot C + A \cdot B \cdot C + A \cdot \bar{B} \cdot \bar{C}$; (d) $(A + B) \cdot (B + C) \cdot (C + A)$.

Answer. The numbers in brackets are those relating to the rules and identities summarized in Table 6.7.

$$
\begin{aligned}
\text{(a)} \quad \bar{A} \cdot \bar{B} + A \cdot \bar{B} &= \bar{B} \cdot \bar{A} + \bar{B} \cdot A & (6) \\
&= \bar{B} \cdot (\bar{A} + A) & (14) \\
&= \bar{B} \cdot 1 & (5) \\
&= \bar{B} & (7)
\end{aligned}
$$

The corresponding truth table is given in Table 6.10.

Table 6.10

A	B	$\bar{A}$	$\bar{B}$	$A \cdot \bar{B}$	$\bar{A} \cdot \bar{B}$	$\bar{A} \cdot \bar{B} + A\bar{B}$
0	0	1	1	0	1	1
0	1	1	0	0	0	0
1	0	0	1	1	0	1
1	1	0	0	0	0	0

It may be seen that the column for $\bar{B}$ is the same as for $\bar{A}\cdot\bar{B} + A\cdot B$ verifying the result. Switch B can be used instead of $A\cdot B + A\cdot B$. Therefore the circuitry involved in the initial system can be considerably simplified giving the same result.

(b)
$$
\begin{aligned}
A\cdot B + A\cdot\bar{B} &= A\,(B + \bar{B}) & (14)\\
&= A\cdot 1 & (5)\\
&= A & (7)
\end{aligned}
$$

It can be seen from Table 6.11 that the columns for A and $A\cdot B + A\cdot\bar{B}$ are the same verifying the result.

Table 6.11

A	B	$\bar{B}$	$A\cdot B$	$A\cdot\bar{B}$	$A\cdot B + A\cdot\bar{B}$
0	0	1	0	0	0
0	1	0	0	0	0
1	0	1	0	1	1
1	1	0	1	0	1

(c)
$$
\begin{aligned}
A\cdot B + A\cdot C + A\cdot B\cdot C + A\cdot\bar{B}\cdot\bar{C} & \\
= A\cdot B\cdot(1 + C) + A\cdot(C + \bar{B}\cdot\bar{C}) & (14)\\
= A\cdot B + A\cdot(C + \bar{B})\cdot(C + \bar{C}) & (2)\,(15)\\
= A\cdot B + A\cdot(C + \bar{B}) & (5)\\
= A\cdot B + A\cdot C + A\cdot\bar{B} & (14)\\
= A\cdot(B + \bar{B}) + A\cdot C & (14)\\
= A + A\cdot C & (5)\\
= A\cdot(1 + C) & (14)\\
= A\cdot 1 & (2)\\
= A & (7)
\end{aligned}
$$

Handwritten annotations to the right:
$A\,(B + c) + A\,(Bc + \bar{B}\bar{c})$
$AB + AC + A\,(\,1\,)$
$AB + AC + A$
$A\,(B + C + 1)$
$A\cdot 1$

In Table 6.12, Z represents the original expression. Since Z and A are equal from the truth table the result is verified.

Table 6.12

A	B	C	$\bar{B}$	$\bar{C}$	$A\cdot B$	$A\cdot C$	$A\cdot B\cdot C$	$A\cdot\bar{B}\cdot\bar{C}$	Z
0	0	0	1	1	0	0	0	0	0
0	0	1	1	0	0	0	0	0	0
0	1	0	0	1	0	0	0	0	0
1	0	0	1	1	0	0	0	1	1
0	1	1	0	0	0	0	0	0	0
1	0	1	1	0	0	1	0	0	1
1	1	0	0	1	1	0	0	0	1
1	1	1	0	0	1	1	1	0	1

$(A + BC)(= (A + B)(A + C)$

66

Rem $(1 + B) A = A$

(d) $(A + B) \cdot (B + C) \cdot (C + A)$

    $= (B + A) \cdot (B + C) \cdot (C + A)$ *inside bracket*   (1)

    $= (B + A \cdot C)(C + A)$ *makes all inside*   (15)

    $= B \cdot (C + A) + A \cdot C \cdot (C + A)$ *bracket = 1*   (14)

multiply by $(C + A)$

    $= B \cdot (C + A) + (A \cdot C) \cdot C + (A \cdot C) A$ (14)

    $= B \cdot (C + A) + A \cdot (C \cdot C) + C \cdot (A \cdot A)$ (6) (13)

    $= B \cdot (C + A) + A \cdot C + C \cdot A$ (9)

    $= B \cdot (C + A) + A \cdot C + A \cdot C$ (6)

    $= B \cdot (C + A) + A \cdot C$ (4)

    $= B \cdot C + B \cdot A + A \cdot C$ (14)

In the truth table depicted in Table 6.13, Z_1 represents the original expression and Z_2 the simplified expression.

Table 6.13

A	B	C	A + B	B + C	C + A	B·C	B·A	A·C	Z_1	Z_2
0	0	0	0	0	0	0	0	0	0	0
0	0	1	0	1	1	0	0	0	0	0
0	1	0	1	1	0	0	0	0	0	0
1	0	0	1	0	1	0	0	0	0	0
0	1	1	1	1	1	1	0	0	1	1
1	0	1	1	1	1	0	0	1	1	1
1	1	0	1	1	1	0	1	0	1	1
1	1	1	1	1	1	1	1	1	1	1

Since Z_1 and Z_2 are the same the result is verified.

Example 2. Modify the Boolean expression $A \cdot B + A \cdot C + B \cdot C$ to give a simpler switching circuit and verify the result using a truth table. Construct the alternative switching circuit.

Answer. $A \cdot B + A \cdot C + B \cdot C = A \cdot (B + C) + B \cdot C$ (14)

    It can be seen from the truth table (Z_1 represents the original expression, Z_2 represents the simplified system) (Table 6.14) that the

Table 6.14

A	B	C	A·B	A·C	B·C	(B + C)	A·(B + C)	Z_1	Z_2
0	0	0	0	0	0	0	0	0	0
0	0	1	0	0	0	1	0	0	0
0	1	0	0	0	0	1	0	0	0
1	0	0	0	0	0	0	0	0	0
0	1	1	0	0	1	1	0	1	1
1	0	1	0	1	0	1	1	1	1
1	1	0	1	0	0	1	1	1	1
1	1	1	1	1	1	1	1	1	1

result is verified. The circuit has been simplified from three branches to two.

The two switching systems are shown in Fig. 6.13.

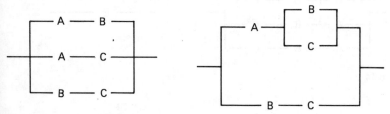

Fig. 6.13

Example 3. Simplify the Boolean expression

$\bar{A} \cdot B \cdot \bar{C} + \bar{A} \cdot B \cdot C + A \cdot B \cdot \bar{C} + A \cdot B \cdot C$

and verify the result using a truth table. Construct the alternative switching circuit.

Answer
$$
\begin{aligned}
\bar{A} \cdot B \cdot \bar{C} &+ \bar{A} \cdot B \cdot C + A \cdot B \cdot \bar{C} + A \cdot B \cdot C \\
&= \bar{A} \cdot B \cdot (\bar{C} + C) + A \cdot B \cdot (\bar{C} + C) &&(14) \\
&= \bar{A} \cdot B \cdot 1 + A \cdot B \cdot 1 &&(5) \\
&= \bar{A} \cdot B + A \cdot B &&(7) \\
&= B \cdot \bar{A} + B \cdot A &&(6) \\
&= B \cdot (\bar{A} + A) &&(14) \\
&= B \cdot 1 &&(5) \\
&= B &&(7)
\end{aligned}
$$

Let Z represent the original expression. It can be seen from the truth table (Table 6.15) that the result is verified.

Table 6.15

A	B	C	$\bar{A}$	$\bar{C}$	$\bar{A} \cdot B \cdot \bar{C}$	$\bar{A} \cdot B \cdot C$	$A \cdot B \cdot \bar{C}$	$A \cdot B \cdot C$	Z
0	0	0	1	1	0	0	0	0	0
0	0	1	1	0	0	0	0	0	0
0	1	0	1	1	1	0	0	0	1
1	0	0	0	1	0	0	0	0	0
0	1	1	1	0	0	1	0	0	1
1	0	1	0	0	0	0	0	0	0
1	1	0	0	1	0	0	1	0	1
1	1	1	0	0	0	0	0	1	1

The two switching systems are shown in Fig. 6.14.

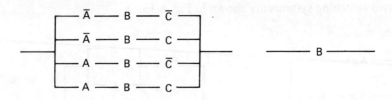

Fig. 6.14

Example 4. Simplify the following Boolean expressions:

(i) $Q\cdot(P\cdot R) + P\cdot(Q\cdot R)$; (ii) $(P + Q)\cdot(P + \bar{Q} + \bar{R})$.

Answer (i) $Q\cdot(P\cdot R) + P\cdot(Q\cdot R)$

$\qquad = Q\cdot P\cdot R + P\cdot Q\cdot R$ (13)

$\qquad = P\cdot Q\cdot R + P\cdot Q\cdot R$ (6)

$\qquad = P\cdot Q\cdot(R + R)$ (14)

$\qquad = P\cdot Q\cdot R$ (4)

(ii) $(P + Q)\cdot(P + \bar{Q} + \bar{R})$

$\qquad = P\cdot P + P\cdot\bar{Q} + P\cdot\bar{R} + Q\cdot P + Q\cdot\bar{Q} + Q\cdot\bar{R}$

$\qquad = P + P\cdot\bar{Q} + P\cdot\bar{R} + Q\cdot P + 0 + Q\cdot\bar{R}$ (9) (10)

$\qquad = (P + 0) + P\cdot\bar{Q} + P\cdot\bar{R} + Q\cdot P + Q\cdot\bar{R}$ (12)

$\qquad = P + P\cdot\bar{Q} + P\cdot Q + P\cdot\bar{R} + Q\cdot\bar{R}$ (3) (6)

$\qquad = P + (P\cdot\bar{Q} + P\cdot Q) + P\cdot\bar{R} + Q\cdot\bar{R}$ (12)

$\qquad = P + P\cdot(\bar{Q} + Q) + P\cdot\bar{R} + Q\cdot\bar{R}$ (14)

$\qquad = P + P\cdot 1 + P\cdot\bar{R} + Q\cdot\bar{R}$ (5)

$\qquad = (P + P) + P\cdot\bar{R} + Q\cdot\bar{R}$ (7) (12)

$\qquad = P + P\cdot\bar{R} + Q\cdot\bar{R}$ (4)

$\qquad = P (1 + \bar{R}) + Q\cdot\bar{R}$ (7) (14)

$\qquad = P\cdot 1 + Q\cdot\bar{R}$ (2)

$\qquad = P + Q\cdot\bar{R}$ (7)

Alternatively:

$\qquad (P + Q)\cdot(P + \bar{Q} + \bar{R})$

$\qquad = (P + Q)\cdot(P + (\bar{Q} + \bar{R}))$ (12)

$\qquad = P + Q\cdot(\bar{Q} + \bar{R})$ (15)

$\qquad = P + Q\cdot\bar{Q} + Q\cdot\bar{R}$ (14)

$\qquad = P + Q\cdot\bar{R}$ (10)

6.4 Karnaugh maps

An alternative method to that of section 6.3 for simplifying Boolean expressions is to use Karnaugh maps. These are particularly valuable when dealing with expressions containing three or four variables. However, in showing how they work let us first consider an expression containing two variables. The truth table given in Table 6.8 represents the expression

$$\overline{A}\cdot\overline{B} + A\cdot\overline{B}$$

Since $A = 0$, $B = 0$, $Z = 1$ in line 1 the square representing this is that in the top left-hand corner of Fig. 6.15 where the value of Z is included. Similarly, $A = 1$, $B = 1$, $Z = 0$ in line 4 is represented by a 0 ($= Z$) in the bottom right-hand corner.

Also $A = 0$, $B = 1$, $Z = 0$ (line 2) appears as 0 in the bottom left-hand corner and $A = 1$, $B = 0$, $Z = 1$ (line 3) appears as 1 in the top right-hand corner. Fig. 6.15 is a Karnaugh map.

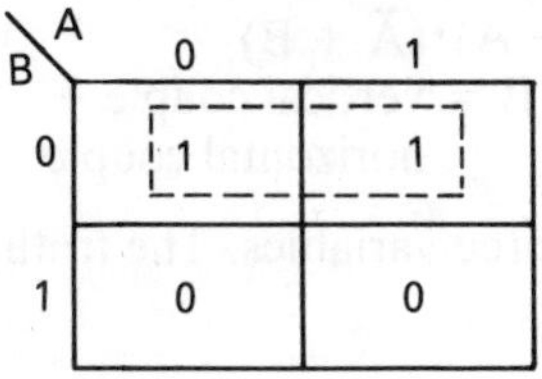

Fig. 6.15

The next stage is to *couple* 1's in adjacent squares horizontally or vertically. For example, a loop has been drawn round the 1's in Fig. 6.15. In this loop $B(= 0)$ is fixed although A varies, i.e. $\overline{B} = 1$. Hence $\overline{A}\cdot\overline{B} + A\cdot\overline{B}$ can be replaced by $\overline{B}$.
Using the method of section 6.3 (Example 1)

$$\overline{A}\cdot\overline{B} + A\cdot\overline{B} = \overline{B}\cdot(\overline{A} + 1) = \overline{B}\cdot 1 = \overline{B} \text{ as above.}$$

Let us now examine the truth table (Table 6.16)

Table 6.16

A	B	Z
0	0	1
0	1	1
1	0	0
1	1	1

70

The corresponding Karnaugh map (Fig. 6.16).

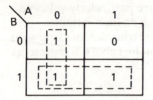

Fig. 6.16

The vertical couple represents $\overline{A}$ ($A = 0$)
The horizontal couple represents B ($B = 1$)
The original expression is (from the truth table)

$$\overline{A} \cdot \overline{B} + \overline{A} \cdot B + A \cdot B$$

On simplification $\overline{A} \cdot (\overline{B} + B) + A \cdot B = \overline{A} + A \cdot B$
$$= (\overline{A} + A) \cdot (\overline{A} + B)$$
$$= \overline{A} + B = \text{vertical couple} +$$
$$\text{horizontal couple}$$

Let us now look at an example involving three variables. The truth table in Table 6.9 represents

$$\overline{A} \cdot B \cdot \overline{C} + A \cdot \overline{B} \cdot \overline{C} + \overline{A} \cdot B \cdot C + A \cdot B \cdot C$$

In the Karnaugh map (Fig. 6.17) the vertical columns represent $A \cdot B$ and the horizontal rows C giving

C\AB	00	01	11	10
0	0	1	0	1
1	0	1	1	0

Fig. 6.17

There are two couples $\overline{A} \cdot B$ ($A = 0$, $B = 1$) and $B \cdot C$ ($B = 1$, $C = 1$) and the final expression is $\overline{A} \cdot B + B \cdot C + A \cdot \overline{B} \cdot \overline{C}$.

Using the methods of section 6.3

$$\overline{A} \cdot B \cdot \overline{C} + \overline{A} \cdot B \cdot C + A \cdot B \cdot C + A \cdot \overline{B} \cdot \overline{C}$$
$$= \overline{A} \cdot B \cdot (\overline{C} + C) + A \cdot B \cdot C + A \cdot \overline{B} \cdot \overline{C}$$
$$= \overline{A} \cdot B + A \cdot B \cdot C + A \cdot \overline{B} \cdot \overline{C}$$
$$= B (\overline{A} + A \cdot C) + A \cdot \overline{B} \cdot \overline{C}$$

$$= B\,(\overline{A} + A)\cdot(\overline{A} + C) + A\cdot\overline{B}\cdot\overline{C}$$
$$= B\,(\overline{A} + C) + A\cdot\overline{B}\cdot\overline{C}$$
$$= \overline{A}\cdot B + B\cdot C + A\cdot\overline{B}\cdot\overline{C}$$

which agrees with the result from the Karnaugh map.

Worked example 6.3.3 involved the simplification of

$$\overline{A}\cdot B\cdot\overline{C} + \overline{A}\cdot B\cdot C + A\cdot B\cdot\overline{C} + A\cdot B\cdot C$$

Using a Karnaugh map (Fig. 6.18) gives

C＼AB	00	01	11	10
0	0	1	1	0
1	0	1	1	0

Fig. 6.18

There are therefore two vertical couples $\overline{A}\cdot B$ (A = 0, B = 1) and $A\cdot B$ (A = 1, B = 1).

There are also two horizontal couples $B\cdot\overline{C}$ (B = 1, C = 0) and $B\cdot C$ (B = 1, C = 1).

Therefore the simplified expression is

$$\overline{A}\cdot B + A\cdot B + B\cdot\overline{C} + B\cdot C$$

which can be simplified further to give

$$B\cdot(\overline{A} + A) + B\cdot(\overline{C} + C) = B + B = B$$

If we now look at the four couples as one group the only common value is B = 1. Hence the overall answer is B. This grouping is quite general.

There is one final point to be considered in the use of Karnaugh maps and this is best seen by use of a simple example.

Simplify $\overline{A}\cdot\overline{B}\cdot\overline{C} + A\cdot\overline{B}\cdot\overline{C}$

The Karnaugh map (Fig. 6.19) is

C＼AB	00	01	11	10
0	1	0	0	1
1	0	0	0	0

Fig. 6.19

We can couple 1's at opposite edges like those in Fig 6.19. The horizontal couple is $\overline{B}\cdot\overline{C}$ (B = 0, C = 0).

Simplifying $\quad \overline{A}\cdot\overline{B}\cdot\overline{C} + A\cdot\overline{B}\cdot\overline{C}$
gives $\qquad\qquad \overline{B}\cdot\overline{C}\cdot(\overline{A} + A)$
$\qquad\qquad\quad = \overline{B}\cdot\overline{C}$ as above

The most valuable use of Karnaugh maps is for variables higher than three where the earlier methods are very cumbersome.

For four variables the columns represent two variables and the rows two variables.

The expression $\overline{A}\cdot\overline{B}\cdot\overline{C}\cdot\overline{D} + A\cdot\overline{B}\cdot\overline{C}\cdot\overline{D} + A\cdot B\cdot C\cdot D + A\cdot\overline{B}\cdot C\cdot D$
$+ A\cdot B\cdot C\cdot\overline{D} + A\cdot\overline{B}\cdot C\cdot\overline{D}$ is given by Fig. 6.20.

CD\AB	00	01	11	10
00	1	0	0	1
01	0	0	0	0
11	0	0	1	1
10	0	0	1	1

Fig. 6.20

There is one group of four in which A = 1 and C = 1, $\therefore$ It is $A\cdot C$
There is one horizontal edge couple in which B = 0 and C = 0, D = 0, $\therefore$ It is $\overline{B}\cdot\overline{C}\cdot\overline{D}$
The simplified expression is $A\cdot C + \overline{B}\cdot\overline{C}\cdot\overline{D}$
This can be verified by the methods of section 6.3.

If we look at Fig. 6.20 we can see that there is a possible couple involving the top and bottom extreme right-hand pairs. These cells have already been used in couples and therefore the resulting term can be ignored. It is called a redundant term. Terms are only redundant if *both* cells of the couple have been previously used.

Worked Examples 6.4

Example 1. Simplify the following examples using Karnaugh maps:

(i) $\overline{A}\cdot B\cdot\overline{C} + \overline{A}\cdot B\cdot C + A\cdot B\cdot C$
(ii) $\overline{A}\cdot\overline{B}\cdot\overline{C} + \overline{A}\cdot\overline{B}\cdot C + \overline{A}\cdot B\cdot C + A\cdot B\cdot C + A\cdot\overline{B}\cdot C$

Answer. (i) The Karnaugh map is given in Fig. 6.21.
It contains one vertical couple $\overline{A}\cdot B$ (A = 0, B = 1)
It also contains one horizontal couple $B\cdot C$ (B = 1, C = 1)

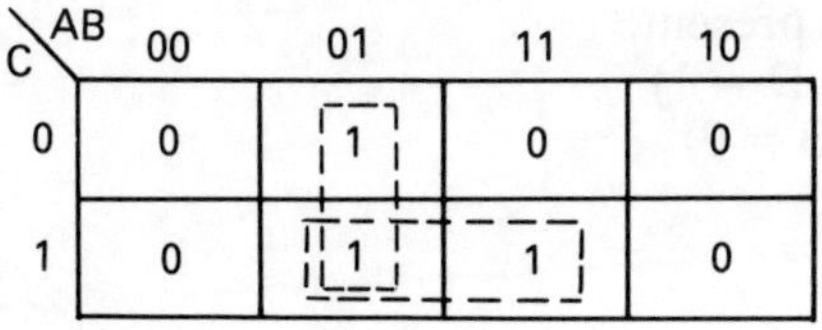

Fig. 6.21

Therefore the simplified expression is

$\overline{A} \cdot B + B \cdot C$

(ii) The Karnaugh map is given in Fig. 6.22.

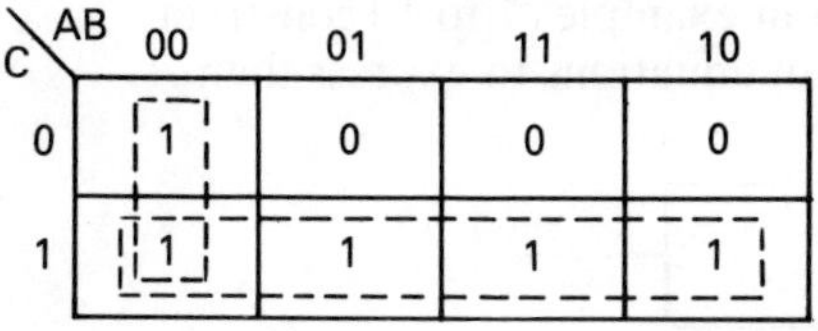

Fig. 6.22

It contains one vertical couple $\overline{A} \cdot \overline{B}$ (A = 0, B = 0)
It also contains one horizontal group of four cells whose only value
which is common is C = 1, therefore it represents C in the same way as
the square group. Therefore the simplified expression is

$\overline{A} \cdot \overline{B} + C$

Example 2. Use a Karnaugh map in order to simplify the following
expression:

$A \cdot \overline{B} \cdot \overline{C} \cdot \overline{D} + A \cdot \overline{B} \cdot \overline{C} \cdot D + A \cdot \overline{B} \cdot C \cdot D + A \cdot \overline{B} \cdot C \cdot \overline{D} + \overline{A} \cdot \overline{B} \cdot \overline{C} \cdot D + \overline{A} \cdot B \cdot \overline{C} \cdot D + \overline{A} \cdot \overline{B} \cdot C \cdot D + \overline{A} \cdot B \cdot C \cdot D$

Answer. The Karnaugh map is given in Fig. 6.23.

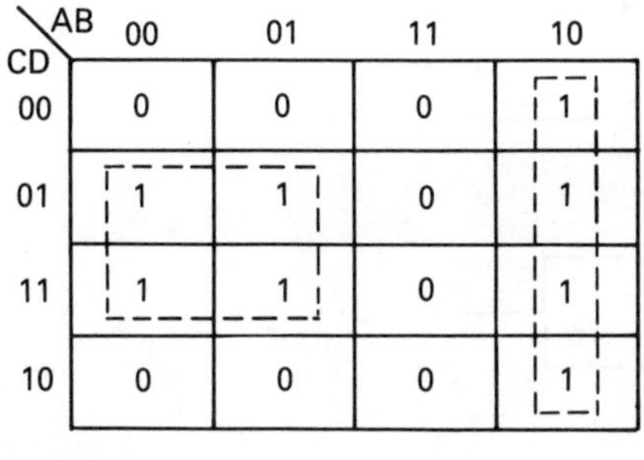

Fig. 6.23

74

There are two groups of four cells present.
The square group is $\bar{A} \cdot D$ (A = 0, D = 1)
The linear group is $A \cdot \bar{B}$ (A = 1, B = 0)
The simplified expression is

$A \cdot \bar{B} + \bar{A} \cdot D$

It would be a useful exercise to check your answers using the methods of Section 6.3.

Exercise 6

Section 6.2

From the switching systems shown in examples 1 to 10 construct suitable logic networks and Boolean equations to express them.

1.

2.

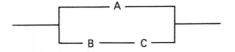

3.

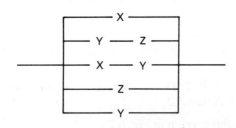

4.

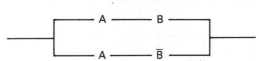

5.

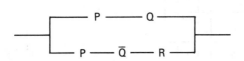

6.

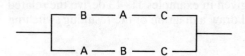

7.

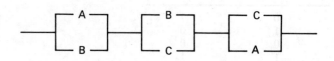

8.

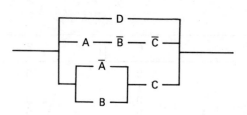

9.

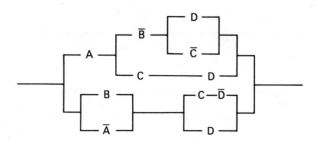

10.

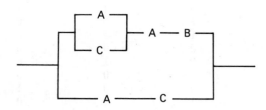

From the truth tables given in examples 11–13 derive the related Boolean equations and draw a diagram of the resulting switching systems.

11. Table 6.17

Table 6.17

A	B	Z
0	0	1
0	1	0
1	0	0
1	1	1

12. Table 6.18

Table 6.18

A	B	C	Z
0	0	0	0
0	0	1	1
0	1	0	0
1	0	0	0
0	1	1	1
1	0	1	1
1	1	0	0
1	1	1	1

13. Table 6.19

Table 6.19

A	B	C	D	Z
0	0	0	0	0
0	0	0	1	1
0	0	1	0	0
0	1	0	0	0
0	0	1	1	1
0	1	0	1	1
0	1	1	0	0
0	1	1	1	0
1	0	0	0	0
1	0	0	1	0
1	0	1	0	0
1	1	0	0	1
1	0	1	1	0
1	1	0	1	0
1	1	1	0	1
1	1	1	1	1

Section 6.3

In the following examples simplify the Boolean expressions as far as possible and confirm the answers by using truth tables.

14. The Boolean expression in examples 3–8 inclusive
15. $A \cdot B \cdot \bar{C} + \bar{C} \cdot \bar{A}$
16. $A \cdot B + \bar{A} \cdot B \cdot C + A \cdot \bar{B} \cdot C + A \cdot B \cdot \bar{C}$
17. $A \cdot (\bar{B}C + \bar{C} \cdot \bar{D}) + B \cdot D (A\bar{C} + \bar{A}) +$
    $C \cdot (B + \bar{D}) + D \cdot (\bar{C} + B \cdot C)] \cdot A$
18. $A \cdot B \cdot C + \bar{B} \cdot C \cdot D + \bar{A} \cdot B \cdot C + \bar{B} \cdot C + \bar{A} \cdot C \cdot D$
19. $(A + \bar{B})(B + \bar{C})(C + \bar{D})(D + \bar{A})$
20. The following statements are an expression of *De Morgan's laws*
    $\overline{A \cdot B} = \bar{A} + \bar{B}$
    $\overline{A + B} = \bar{A} \cdot \bar{B}$
    Confirm the truth of these laws using truth tables.

Section 6.4

21. Repeat examples 14–19 using Karnaugh maps to obtain your simplified expression in each case.
22. Simplify the following expression by means of a Karnaugh map:

$\bar{A} \cdot \bar{B} \cdot \bar{C} \cdot \bar{D} + \bar{A} \cdot \bar{B} \cdot \bar{C} \cdot D + A \cdot \bar{B} \cdot \bar{C} \cdot \bar{D} + A \cdot \bar{B} \cdot \bar{C} \cdot D + \bar{A} \cdot B \cdot C \cdot D +$
$A \cdot B \cdot C \cdot D + \bar{A} \cdot B \cdot C \cdot \bar{D} + A \cdot B \cdot C \cdot \bar{D}$

Appendix

International (MIL) logic symbols

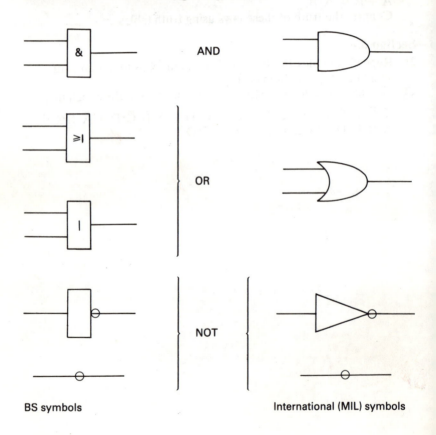

BS symbols   International (MIL) symbols

Answers

Chapter 1

1. 100111, 1110101, 100101010, 1010001110, 10000000101,
   11111011000, 1011010001, 1111100111, 1010100000, 101111001011
2. 0.11, 0.011, 0.0001, 0.10001, 0.00011, 0.11111, 0.0011
3. 0.11011, 0.11101, 0.11001, 0.11010, 0.00110
4. 10011.0001, 11000.1111, 1100110.0010, 11100111.1111,
   100111010.0111, 1010000010.0101, 1000000000.1100
5. 3, 5, 15, 93, 99, 65, 221, 31, 39, 115
6. 0.25, 0.75, 0.6875, 0.90625, 0.53125, 0.0625, 0.4375
7. 3.5, 5.625, 7.875, 9.1875, 10.5, 8.6875, 29.03125, 8.0625
9. 011001110100.100, 001001010000011.110011110,
   010001100001110.101010

Chapter 2

1. (1) 111, (2) 1111, (3) 1011, (4) 10100, (5) 11110, (6) 1001010,
   (7) 1101101, (8) 110000, (9) 1101011, (10) 1000111
2. (1) 1.0000, (2) 0.1100, (3) 1.10000, (4) 1.00010, (5) 1.010110,
   (6) 0.1100000
3. (1) 110.011, (2) 1100.111, (3) 11001.010, (4) 100110.1110,
   (5) 1110000.10000, (6) 100111110.110011
4. (1) 01011, (2) 01101, (3) 00011, (4) 0110, (5) 0010110, (6) 10110
   (01001), (7) 11110 (00001), (8) 001101, (9) 1101110 (0010001),
   (10) 00110 Bracketed figures are ones complements
5. (1) 01.10, (2) 011.100, (3) 0010.1001, (4) 100110.0011,
   (5) 10100.0010, (6) 11101.00101
6. (1) 1000, (2) 1111, (3) 1110101, (4) 11100001, (5) 11111100,
   (6) 11100100, (7) 110010000, (8) 100001010
7. (1) 101101.00011, (2) 1101.111011, (3) 1111.110111,
   (4) 1001000010.110111
8. (1) 101, (2) 1000, (3) 1111, (4) 100 (rem = 10011), (5) 110
   (rem = 11), (6) 10001 (rem = 10001)
9. (1) 100.01 (2) 1.1, (3) 1101.1, (4) 11.11
10. (1) 101.00101, (2) 111.10001, (3) 1110.11101, (4) 1111.11001

Chapter 3

1. (1) −12, (2) +12, (3) +5, (4) + 25, (5) −1, (6) + 10, (7) −21, (8) −29, (9) −25, (10) +18
2. (1) 0010101, 0010110, (2) 1001011, 1001100, (3) 11000111, 11001000, (4) 01101001, 01101010, (5) 000010101, 000010110, (6) 01011110, 01011111

Chapter 4

1. (a)

X	Y	Lamp
0	0	1
0	1	1
1	0	1
1	1	0

(b)

A	B	Lamp
0	0	1
0	1	0
1	0	0
1	1	0

(c)

A	B	C	Lamp
0	0	0	0
0	0	1	1
0	1	0	0
1	0	0	0
0	1	1	1
1	0	1	1
1	1	0	1
1	1	1	1

(d)

A	B	C	Lamp
0	0	0	0
0	0	1	0
0	1	0	0
1	0	0	0
0	1	1	1
1	0	1	1
1	1	0	0
1	1	1	1

(e)

P	Q	R	Lamp
0	0	0	1
0	0	1	1
0	1	0	1
1	0	0	1
0	1	1	0
1	0	1	0
1	1	0	1
1	1	1	0

Inverse of (d))

(f)

P	Q	R	Lamp
0	0	0	1
0	0	1	0
0	1	0	1
1	0	0	1
0	1	1	0
1	0	1	0
1	1	0	0
1	1	1	0

Inverse of (c))

Chapter 5

In questions 1–4 let a and b be the individual propositions and let z be the compound proposition.

1. $z = a + b$ 2. $z = a + b$ 3. $z = a \cdot b$ 4. $z = a \cdot b$
9. (a) $Z = \overline{X \cdot Y}$, (b) $Z = \overline{A + B}$, (c) $Z = A \cdot B + C$, (d) $Z = (A + B) \cdot C$, (e) $Z = \overline{(P + Q) \cdot R}$, (f) $Z = \overline{P \cdot Q + R}$

Chapter 6

1.

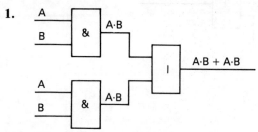

$A \cdot B + A \cdot B = 1$

2.

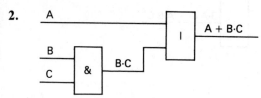

$A + B \cdot C = 1$

3.

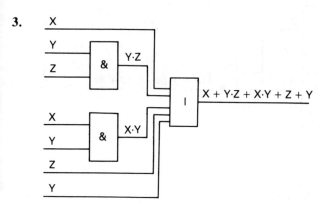

$X + Y \cdot Z + X \cdot Y + Z + Y = 1$

4.

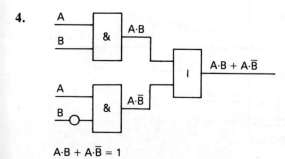

$A \cdot B + A \cdot \overline{B} = 1$

5.

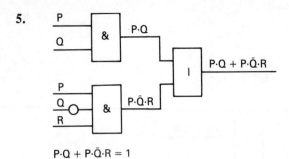

$P \cdot Q + P \cdot \bar{Q} \cdot R = 1$

6.

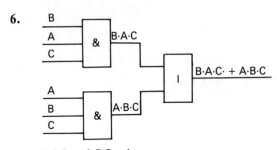

$B \cdot A \cdot C. + A \cdot B \cdot C = 1$

7.

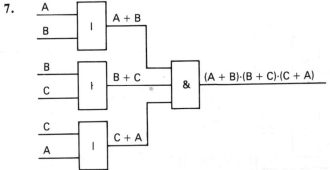

$(A + B) \cdot (B + C) \cdot (C + A) = 1$

8.

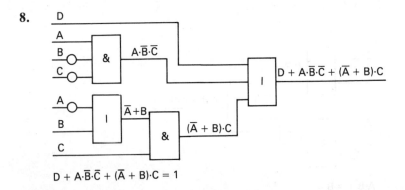

$D + A \cdot \bar{B} \cdot \bar{C} + (\bar{A} + B) \cdot C = 1$

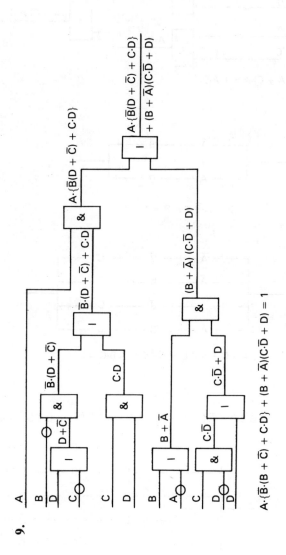

9.

$$A \cdot \{\overline{B} \cdot (B + \overline{C}) + C \cdot D\} + (B + \overline{A})(C \cdot \overline{D} + D) = 1$$

83

10.

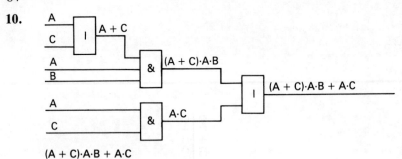

$(A + C) \cdot A \cdot B + A \cdot C$

11.

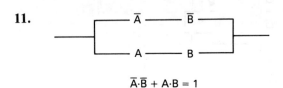

$\overline{A} \cdot \overline{B} + A \cdot B = 1$

12.

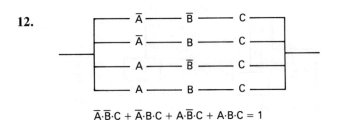

$\overline{A} \cdot \overline{B} \cdot C + \overline{A} \cdot B \cdot C + A \cdot \overline{B} \cdot C + A \cdot B \cdot C = 1$

13. $\overline{A} \cdot \overline{B} \cdot \overline{C} \cdot D + \overline{A} \cdot \overline{B} \cdot C.D + \overline{A} \cdot B \cdot \overline{C} \cdot D + A \cdot B \cdot \overline{C} \cdot \overline{D} + A \cdot B \cdot C \cdot \overline{D} + A \cdot B \cdot C \cdot D = 1$

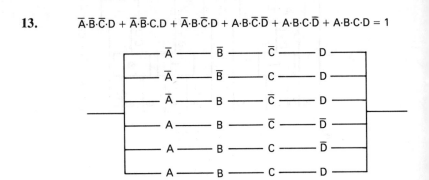

14. X + Y + Z, A, P·(Q + R), A·B·C, A·B + B·C + C·A, No
    simplification

15. $\overline{C}·(B + \overline{A})$

16. A·B + B·C + C·A

17. A + B·D + B·D·$\overline{C}$ + A·C·$\overline{D}$

18. C + $\overline{A}$C·D

19. A·B·C·D + $\overline{A}·\overline{B}·\overline{C}·\overline{D}$

21. B·C + $\overline{B}·\overline{C}$

Index